The Originals

Maximilian Press Publishers

The Originals

By

Doris C. Baker

The Originals
By Doris C. Baker

Published and Manufactured by
Maximilian Press Publishers
920 South Battlefield Boulevard,
Chesapeake, Virginia 23322
757-482-2273

Maximilian Press and colophon are registered trademarks
Of Maximilian Press Publishers

Cover art work by John Walker
Edited by Marc Daniels

First Printing: June 2002

Manufactured in the United States of America

10 09 08 07 06 05 04 03 02 01

Library of Congress Catalogue Number Pending

Baker, Doris C.

       The Originals: A Novel / Doris C. Baker
       p.   cm

       1. Novel. 2. U. S. Army Special Forces 3. Green Berets.
       4. Bad Tölz, Germany. 5. Department of Defense. 6. U. S. Army Schools.
       7. Military. 8. Hungary. 9. Vietnam. 10. Fiction. I. Title.

ISBN 1-930211-38-4

This book has been composed in Times New Roman

The paper used in this publication meets the minimum requirements
of ANSI/NISO Z39.48-1992 (R1997)

Dedication
For Evelyn and the Green Berets

FROM THE AUTHOR

Special forces are now in the media limelight, and my novel, The Originals, a semi- finalist in the 1997 William Faulkner Literary competition, is a book which has found its time. It begins in the uneasy aftermath of World War II, a time of shifting, settling, and upheaval, temporary threats to world peace, the Hungarian Revolution, the Vietnam War and the murder of JFK. The story reflects related changes in the lives of the first soldiers who formed the 10th Special Forces Group Airborne, soldiers President Kennedy named the Green Berets.

The Originals will appeal to readers of literary fiction as well as Special Forces personnel and, in the light of their present mission, many others both here and overseas who are interested in their history.

As principal of an American School in Bad Tölz, Germany I knew the original Green Berets for more than twenty years from the first moment when their advance party strode into the Park Hotel Officer's Club as if they owned the place. In the book their voices are authentic. Most of the locales and a few characters and incidents are real. The rest are consistent with what happened. Although war scenes are part of the background, it is essentially the story of Kate O'Brien, an American woman who is caught in the dangerous lives and fortunes of these extraordinary men.

Doris C. Baker

PREFACE

A love affair as clandestine as the founding and operation of the Special Forces (SF) at Flint Kaserne, Bad Tölz, Germany in 1953. Kate O'Brien, a Department of Defense (DOD) school teacher befriends SF personnel and shares multiple experiences enveloping their wants, desires, and most of all, their fears and heroism. Ivan is one of those officers who finds great difficulty in exposing his affection and love until he is about to transfer into the jungles of Vietnam.

The Originals forces you to turn the pages to discover the profundity and courage of both Kate and Ivan in their final acceptance. A memorable read.

William A. Hamel, Ph.D.
Psychologist - Publisher
Maximilian Press Publishers

Acknowledgements

THE ORIGINALS

Acknowledgements:

One of those fortuitous circumstances that compels authors to write books, sent me in the early Fifties to Bad Tölz, Germany, the first overseas base of the 10th Special Forces Group Airborne, later Green Berets. These extraordinary men and their women seemed like exotic actors in a Hollywood movie, irresistible source material for a novel. My characters thank them for various disguises and borrowed conversations.

Among others who shared the Bad Tölz Era, Evelyn Thimedes, Matt Gately, Caesar Civitella, and John Scagnelli deserve special recognition for memories and encouragement which helped me years later to write THE ORIGINALS.

I am especially indebted to my gifted editor, Sofia Starnes, for her intuitive understanding of my characters, their motivations, and the inevitable direction of their story. My essay, The Green Berets, would not have become a book without her expert guidance. The Thursday Poets' interest as the work progressed gave me information for the Hungarian Revolution chapters.

The following books furnished background material for Hungarian and Vietnam scenes: Charles M. Simpson III USA (Ret.), *Inside the Green Berets* (1983); W.E.B. Griffen, *The Berets, Brotherhood of War* (1985); Robin Moore, *The Green Berets,* (novel) 1965; James Michener, *The Bridge at Andau,* 1957; Noel Barber, *Seven Days of Freedom, The Hungarian Uprising 1956,* 1974; Reg Gadney, *Cry Hungary,* 1986; Richard S. Esbenshade, *Cultures of the World, Hungary,* 1994.

A well written, authentic piece of work, full of insights into the world of the Green Berets. Reading was like walking again the streets of Visegrad, in Hungary.

Frank Schatz, Columnist
The Virginia Gazette

The Originals brings back memories of extraordinary people and times.

Evelyn Thimedes
Teacher in Tölz, 1954 - 1982

There was a time, there was a place, there were a number of unique individuals whose lives impacted ours. Yet, they remained essentially their own, apart. Author Doris Baker partook intimately of those lives and, in her deeply human and engaging work, she makes them personally relevant to us. Through its succinct, natural prose and underlying poetry, this book makes us grateful we once knew The Originals, or utterly regretful that we never did.

Sofia M. Starnes, Author
The Soul's Landscape,
A Commerce of Moments

The Originals tells a compelling story of the United States Army Green Berets with a different slant. The author knows her subject.

Matt Gately, Colonel, United States Army
One of the originals, Fort Bragg 1952

The men of the Green Berets are forever etched in my mind for they instilled my reason for existence. Munich '53, Frankfurt '54, Bay of Pigs '61, Cholon, Saigon, Bien Hoa, Hoa Cam and Danang '61 - '63.

William Hamel, Ph.D.
Maximilian Press Publishers

CHAPTER ONE

It was pure nightmare. The Chinks were attacking his company from all sides like furies from hell. In a double flashback he dived into a foxhole, then suddenly, changed into a prisoner jolting along a dirt road with three Nazi officers. Ivan woke up in a sweat, shivering. For an instant, reaching for his gun, he thought he was back in Korea. A loose branch on the lean-to was letting in a shower of snow. He crawled out of his sleeping bag and poked it back into position, swearing.

Arriving in 1955 for a tour with the elite 10th Special Forces in Bad Tölz, Germany, Captain Robert Herrick, called Ivan by his friends, had a week or so of sound sleep before the nightmares came back. He wasn't the only one of the SFs to wake up in the middle of a snow bank on maneuvers in the Bavarian Mountains, muttering in his sleep, endlessly fighting in past battlefields. They never talked about such episodes, although they were closer than most brothers. And he did not mention it to Kate.

A third grade teacher in the American School, Kate was the only woman Ivan knew who showed no interest in him except for a meeting of minds. Their relationship was filled with ups and downs from the start. He had a Don Quixote complex quite apart from his military career where he was known for cool concentration. He longed with evangelical fervor to help women develop into the goddesses they really were. By the time Ivan came to Bad Tölz, he had already married and divorced one of them. He never failed to be surprised when his particular idea of a goddess didn't materialize. No matter how many art exhibitions and Vivaldi recordings he brought into their relationship, it often refused to turn into a Pygmalion drama.

A few of his women were as brilliant as he

was, and that ruined everything. At first he was
proud—"See what I have wrought!"—But soon
the threats to his ego became irksome.
Despondency and alcohol set in resulting in last
suppers with no regrets on either side.

One fall evening after an arduous day of
training, thirsty and ready for some conversation
and perhaps, if he had timed it right, supper,
Ivan's first sally was, "What do you think of
Sartre?" She was looking for Parmesan cheese
and didn't immediately reply. "Bet you never
heard of him. My God, and you're a school
teacher!"

"Is he a football player?" Kate asked inno-
cently. Seeing his incredulous expression, "Why
don't you ask Beauvoir? She thinks he's quite
nice. At least they both exist and that's important—for them anyway."

"That is positively the damnedest answer I
ever got to a question, and I've heard a few!
Okay. Let's try again. How about Socrates, or
was he before your time?"

"Hm-m-m." She took the spoon out of a pot
on the stove. "He was pretty smart, wasn't he?
On the other hand, he did drink hemlock, or was
that Diogenes?"

"I give up," Ivan groaned. "You're in some
kind of a mood!" and he sat down to a heaping
plate of spaghetti and a bottle of beer. Much later
they were still warring over Sartre and Socrates,
but Ivan was becoming less interested in the
subject. She encouraged him to go home. "Who
cares?" Ivan muttered as he went out the door.

Kate O'Brien was in her middle twenties,
tall with dark auburn hair, gray eyes that sometimes turned green, and a generous mouth—not
exactly pretty, but charming with the rare ability
to make life more exciting than it usually is. Her
third graders in the American Dependents
School found learning irresistible. There was
something about the way she gave them half-
used crayons or an extra piece of newsprint for

rewards that seemed as special as a Pulitzer prize to her eight-year-olds.

Besides the children, all sorts of people were attracted to Kate. She was a good listener, as attentive as their own mothers, which is a powerful magnet for just about anybody's inner child. They told her secrets they had never before divulged, and Kate never revealed what she knew, however breath-taking.

The next evening, Kate was finishing the dishes when she heard loud banging. It had to be Ivan. She wiped her hands and opened the door. "Are we going to reveal our innermost thoughts?" She raised her eyebrows. "If so, you go first."

Ivan looked pleased and set the bottle he had brought on the kitchen table, reaching for a glass in the cupboard. "I already know your problems. Anyway, mine are more interesting." He followed her into the living room, took off his jump boots, and flopped on the sofa with a sigh, half closing his eyes. She thought, with any luck he'd soon be snoozing. Instead he sat up and put on a recording of *Carmina Burana*, turning it to full volume. During one of the softer interludes Ivan ventured for no apparent reason, "You know everything. I suppose you know one of our guys has this friendship with Frieda."

Kate considered and finally agreed she'd heard about Frieda. "Everybody knows Frieda."

"Not everybody. Just one at the moment. She's a damned nice woman—older—, God, she must be over forty—but all cats are black in the dark. And they're so grateful!" Kate looked interested, which encouraged Ivan to believe he had her complete attention. "She's skinny, greenish, like Mildred in *Of Human Bondage* I guess, but nice—really! They say no money's involved but she shares what's in the cupboard."

"The way to a man's heart," Kate murmured.

"Am I boring you? What'd you say?"

"Nothing."

"Oh, the guys take her cigarettes, coffee, whatever—other stuff."

"I hope the guy on duty takes her more than that, if he's the only one!"

"Of course he does. After he goes there'll be somebody else to look out for her. That's understood."

"Aren't you all being a little cold-blooded? Passing her around like an old football? I hear some of the fellows call her Mattress Back."

"Well, Damn it, I don't." Ivan was aggravated, scowling. "It's not like that for the ones who know her. You don't understand, but then, in your teachery insulated environment, it's to be expected! Some women do more than talk. They're warm, consenting adults!"

"Guess so. Must try harder in the future." She yawned. Ivan looked at her suspiciously, and she added, "But how do you explain I'm listening to your worldly tale? Oops! That's the wrong word. All this preoccupation with sex. Is *Carmina Burana* that erotic?"

Ivan looked self-satisfied. "You're not getting any younger you know!" He squinted at her, obviously ready to launch into a lengthy monologue.

"Something happened at school today that will give you a laugh," Kate said, before he could begin.

"No it won't. But fire away if you must."

"All right—if you're going to be like that!"

"No, really. I'm all ears."

"Yes, they are large—. Anyway, your beret won't ever fall down over your eyes!"

Now he was getting irritated. She thought bringing his beret into the conversation probably wasn't such a good idea.

"Oh, for God's sake, get on with it!"

Kate's voice was soothing. "Picture all twenty seven of my little darlings sitting on the floor, looking up at me as if I'm the font of all knowledge. I notice the scraggly geraniums along the windowsill, and a story for all those little faces pops into my head. Are you listening?" Ivan nodded, scowling.

"Okay, here goes. 'I read in a newspaper somewhere—I don't know if it's true—that plants grow better and have shiny leaves and prettier flowers if we talk to them nicely. Maybe it makes them happy.'

"All the turned-up faces are looking at me, and it's hard to tell if these worldly army offspring really believe me. Some of them look pretty skeptical—the ones who will grow up to be scientists. Mary Ann asks, 'Is that really true, Miss O'Brien?' Of course I tell them, 'I don't know. What do you think?' Ivan fidgeted, planting his feet firmly as if to stand up.

"Later that day I notice shy quiet Bobby, whose seat is by the windows, gazing at a half-dead geranium beside him. He seems to be in deep thought. Looking around to be sure nobody is watching, he whispers to the geranium, 'Hello there.'" Kate paused to see what Ivan thought of her school anecdote.

His only comment was, "Some of our conversations, Babe, can only be described as surreal," but his expression was warm, a bit fatherly, Kate thought, and there was a touch of admiration in his smile as he put on his jump boots. "Are you sure you aren't a reincarnation of Paul Bunyan?"

"Not my style," said Kate. He really had liked her story. "Wanna hear another good yarn? And it's absolutely true, on my honor."

"No!" Ivan backed away hastily and stopped by the door to finish lacing his boots. "Your stories are trumped up, shameless prevarications, and you know it." He stood up.

She laughed. "You're fu-u-nny. I learned it from you."

He gave her a quizzical, one-sided grin and rolled his eyes in mock despair.

"Good night." She yawned again.

She heard him mutter under his breath, "Oh shit," as the door closed.

By October 1956, there were signs of coming events in Flint Kaserne, the American Base outside Bad Tölz. A group of senators flew into the airstrip for a brief visit to Headquarters Company, plus the fringe benefits of PX shopping and a weekend in Garmisch. The men were called out on alert no more frequently than usual, but there were daily briefings on the Hungarian Uprising.

Captain Robert "Ivan" Herrick and two sergeants, Ed Kish and John Sepeshy, were the Hungarian language specialists in the Group, and the heat was on their A Team. If Americans went into Hungary their Special Forces team was scheduled for infiltration behind enemy lines. Once in, they would have no one to depend on except themselves, although there were CIA contacts, one in Visegrad, a fortress town on the Danube, and three in Budapest—hardly reliable cover. Other members of the Special Forces A team were: demolition experts—Kish was one of them—, medics including Sep, radio techs, crack weapons men, two intelligence sergeants, and a team master sergeant. All of them were cross-trained in case of need.

Special Forces partying reached new heights, living it up, drowning bad dreams in liquor and laughs. A crowd of single officers, couples, and teachers often gathered in Kate's apartment after the SFs had "dropped" into the airstrip from Neubiberg or Grafenwöhr or Berlin. There was nothing unusual about their absences or returns now—nothing but palpable, building tension in the air.

On rare occasions Kate longed for a little peace and quiet away from the American Dependents School and the problems and intricacies of her friends' lives. The weekend of October 20th was one of those occasions. An

early snow covered the Hohemunde and came
down the Isar Valley frosting the top of the
Blomberg. Most of the teachers had gone to
Garmisch. Kate decided to stay home and was
piled up in bed with a stack of books from the
post library, when she heard a knock on the door.

Charlie, a short nondescript man with rim-
less glasses, followed Ivan. Ivan was in a strange
mood and appeared to be sober. It seemed that
Charlie was from D.C., connected with the
Department of Defense and just passing through
on a fact-finding mission. "Fact-finding about
what?" Kate wanted to know.

Ivan coughed or it could have been a laugh,
and Charlie hesitated for a split second. "Oh,
troop morale, training, and equipment." He lit
his cigar, which seemed to go out frequently, letting bits of wet stump fall on the carpet. Kate
decided he was a revolting little man and gave
Ivan the high sign to take him away, which he
ignored. While she was in the kitchen pouring
drinks, Charlie's voice, barely audible, made her
prick up her ears. "So, Ivan, do you need back-
up or more time?"

Kate couldn't hear what Ivan answered, but
he sounded cross. "Right," Charlie continued.
"Remember that Zoltan is totally unreliable, but
we can't ditch him."

"You think I'm stupid?" With that loud
remark, Ivan came out in the kitchen to get the
drinks. "Charlie here thinks I don't know
Munich is full of Frauleins. I know the names of
at least half of 'em! ALL of 'em in the Dolly
Bar!"

Charlie smiled bleakly, wiping his glasses
and stubbing out his dead cigar at the same time.
He stood up, saying he was tired, and when Ivan
made no move to go, took a long swig of his
drink, thanked Kate for her hospitality, and left.

"Well, I'm glad that creep is gone!" Kate
scowled. "Are you supposed to be his mother or
something?"

"More the other way around," answered Ivan. "He's a leg, but he's got some good points even if he doesn't jump out of airplanes. He can drive a car backwards at sixty miles an hour. Maybe I'll try that myself some day."

The next day in late afternoon Ivan came by Kate's quarters with Durwood, his German shepherd, and a bag of dog food, asking her to keep the dog for a few days until he came back.

"Exactly how long?" Kate wanted to know.

"I dunno—maybe Thursday," Ivan said, giving Durwood a pat on the head. And then without a look back, he walked away.

"Guess I'm elected," she muttered. "There's something persuasive about a Green Beret and jump boots! So handsome! Good I like dogs, Woody ol' boy, or you'd have to go live with those man-eating K-9s out at Lenggries. C'mon!" Durwood looked expectantly at the bag of food and followed Kate inside. She took his bowl out of the cupboard, filled it and set it under the kitchen table where he always ate when he was visiting.

The Föhn, a warm wind blowing down from the mountains, took away the skim of early snow. A gloomy evening settled over the valley and Kate's head began to ache. She went to bed early, feeling uneasy, but her eyes would not stay closed. Sometime during the night, the dog curled up on the foot of the bed and they both slept.

CHAPTER TWO

The night before shots were fired into the crowd around Radio Budapest, Ivan, Kish, and Sep left a valley among low hills west of Visegrad, Hungary's old fortress town on the Danube Bend. By the time they reached its outskirts, the western horizon had darkened from a line of brilliant blood red to black and thunderclouds were rolling up, covering the first glimmer of stars.

"Jól van, Giúk." Ivan's voice was low. He was speaking Magyarul, Hungarian with a country flavor, a dialect fairly similar all over Hungary. "First we stash this stuff in a safe place. Then it's time to separate." They were passing an old cemetery. "I'll guarantee nobody's coming here tonight." The other two nodded and grinned. The captain's village accent was getting richer with every word. It boded well for the mission, and they could use some luck if the other members of the team weren't waiting for them in Budapest.

In a few minutes their small cache of supplies was stowed below the projecting roof of an old chapel discolored by ancient mold. The dim light of a street lamp cast haphazard cross-shadows on gravestones and iron fretwork. Carefully tended plants grew in small rectangular plots. They spoke of generations of families who had lived and died in Visegrad. Partly visible photos of the deceased on their markers, a congregation of silent people, peered at the SFs from deepening shadows.

Ivan and Sep seemed unmoved by their surroundings, but Kish had a sudden vision of his mother who had been born in a village near Visegrad. He stumbled over a headstone on a baby's grave and barely saved himself by grabbing the arm of a stone angel.

Barring a flood, their cache would stay dry and unnoticed by passersby until it was needed.

As they walked out of the cemetery, Ivan reminded them, "Stay within sight and keep your noses clean. If you get in trouble, try to come back here. We'll look for an empty shed on the way in, closer to Zoltan's, but this'll be our back-up."

Keeping distance between them, the SFs left the newer part of Visegrad and aimed toward the old town and the Danube. There was nothing in their appearance to suggest they were Americans. The few people they met on the street passed by in a hurry to reach home before the rain came, and took no notice of them. Now the cobblestone streets narrowed and the houses were one-story with tile roofs. The brick and mortar walls showed the accumulation of years they had stood below the fortress.

Sep thought of his grandmother's stories of her childhood in Hungary—how they spent winters in the warm kitchen, safe from cold winds blowing down off the Börzsöny Mountains or from the Puszta, the Great Plains of Hungary.

In the summer his grandmother remembered sunny days playing jacks with colored pebbles in the courtyard surrounded by the walls of her home. In the evenings they listened to moths plopping to their death in the oil lamp on the supper table. She often told Sep about her father who liked to sit with her brothers on the bench by the front door after supper. He'd smoke his pipe until it was late and time to go to bed.

When pears and plums were ripe in the garden, the old man made schnapps. Once he was smoking, leaning over a huge kettle containing the last stage of the process, which was almost pure alcohol. In the explosion his eyebrows were singed and his whiskers burned completely off. From then on he left the details to his wife who was blessed with a great deal of common sense.

After this story Sep's grandmother always added proudly, "My father's nature was that of an artist. He covered every scrap of paper he could find with sketches as delicate and complicated as spider webs."

Sep brought himself sharply back to the present. Now the benches were empty and few lights showed on the street side of the houses. Their walls were drawn in around central courtyards, the only sign of life, a pungent smell of cooking, the aroma of paprika, garlic, and onions.

The clouds parted a little and the dark bulk of the fortress ruins loomed above the river. It thundered in the distance and Kish shivered. He was a short, jolly man who loved to joke, but in spite of his reputation in Special Forces as a prankster, he was more conventional than most of the singles. He was seriously looking for someone with whom to build his life. Kish wasn't handsome. He did have a good, dependable, rather broad face, and his short legs supported a strong muscular body. In school as he was growing up, the girls hadn't noticed him much, which was just as well. His father and mother, Hungarian immigrants, owned a small farm near Detroit and kept him too busy with chores for any socializing after school. His father's weak heart made it necessary for Ed to take over most of the heavy work on the farm when he was only fifteen. It was a rare event when he went to a class party, and anyway he didn't feel comfortable in clothes he otherwise wore only to church on Sunday.

Kish joined the army soon after his parents died and now he was happier than he had ever been, even though this risky mission had its drawbacks. He wondered briefly what his parents would think of this adventure in their native land.

More than half their Special Forces team was missing and the three men were in no mood to joke. The mission was in trouble, and it was only the beginning. They said nothing to each other about their prospects, but their faces were grim.

The first big drops hit the ground and they hurried toward the Danube and Zoltan's house. The directions were: near the lower castle, Solomon's Tower, then turn toward the river on Fö Utca. Sep found a tumbledown shed in a mostly empty area near their destination, and Ivan followed him in, signaling Kish to join them.

When they were all inside, Ivan asked Kish, "At the briefings, did you get enough info to handle the first contact with Zoltan?"

"Affirmative!" answered Kish. What's the matter with the ol' man? He knows perfectly well I know the routine! I must look even more simple-minded than usual! The three men picked their way out of woodpiles and debris in the shed.

Zoltan had been recruited years before by the Agency. A great shaggy man with a drooping mustache and fierce eyes from his Magyar ancestors, he loathed the Nazis because of the scar on his granddaughter's face. Now he was wary of Communists and government in general, switching allegiance when expedient. It was a natural matter of survival in a country overrun for almost a thousand years by Mongolian Tartars, Turks, the Hapsburgs, Nazis, and most recently, Russians. Sometimes these changes left him on the wrong side. Just now he was an unwilling tool of the AVOs, the Hungarian Secret Police, and there was a reason for that too.

A far-sighted man, Zoltan had begun teaching his granddaughter, Vera, very early in her life how to survive in the changing fortunes of their country. At first, after the Nazi horror, Communists had seemed like benefactors to what was left of his family, but it soon became apparent they were much like the former regime. Now the Americans. It was well to be vigilant

and talk as little as possible, while pretending to
cooperate with your audience at the moment.
Right now he and Vera, especially his beautiful
Vera, were subject to the whims of the local
Communists.

The AVOs, his own countrymen, were much
more of a danger than the Russians. Best to keep
them mollified by offering them American tid-
bits. Whatever it took to protect Vera, he would
do even at the cost of his own life. He must give
her every benefit of his experience as a double
agent, now that she was a woman.

Zoltan heard three knocks. His hands trembled as he set down his glass of wine. He picked
up a lantern and went to the door without haste,
giving himself time, thinking he was getting too
old for this business. He peered out. The young
man standing there asked in peasant Hungarian
if he had a room for the night. As was required,
he replied, "Yes, in the loft above the kitchen."

"Will it be warm?"

"Of course," answered Zoltan. Kish went in,
hand on the gun under his rain gear. Noticing,
Zoltan added, "I live alone except for my granddaughter." He paused. "Vera knows nothing
about my connections. Right now she's taking
some chicken soup to her godmother who's
sick."

Kish wasn't happy to hear about the granddaughter—another complication. Zoltan led him
through the entry into the kitchen, closed the
shutters overlooking the courtyard, and they sat
down on a bench by the table, Kish facing the
door. Zoltan offered him a token glass of pálin-
ka. Kish accepted, relishing its fiery afterglow.
Probably Zoltan had made it himself from the
pear trees in his garden. When Kish was growing up in Michigan, his own grandfather had dis-
tilled the same kind of brandy.

There was a wood fire in the stove and the
kitchen was redolent with strings of peppers and
garlic that hung from low ceiling beams. Fall

apples were drying on shelves, chairs, and every
flat place available, their spicy scent mingling
with other earthy odors.

The two men began to discuss contacts in
Budapest, likely scenarios for the unrest, and
vulnerable key positions in the city. Finally,
Zoltan's eyes narrowed to slits. "I thought there
were supposed to be more of you. Is America
with us or not?"

"We had to leave in a hurry," Kish evaded
the question. "There's one more. It'll take a little time to bring him in," adding, "We value your
information." Suspicion faded from the older
man's eyes replaced by a flash of cunning,
which Kish noted as he went out into the darkness. He walked a few steps and stopped, listening. The rain had become a fine mist, slicking
the cobblestones. Streets were deserted and
there was no sound except a boat bobbing
against a dock somewhere near.

Ivan and Sep were waiting in the shadows
behind Zoltan's house. They returned to the shed
and Kish filled them in about the granddaughter,
and the fact that Zoltan had denied there was an
outpost of the AVO in the fortress, in spite of
rumors to the contrary.

Ivan scowled and shook his head in disgust.
"Better get the hell out of here. We're too
damned conspicuous in this little place-nobody
to watch our backs. Where the hell are they? In
Budapest ahead of us for Christ sake?" They
checked their watches. It was too late for stragglers to be out. The three men walked back sep-
arately to the cemetery and picked up their supplies.

Sep was a tall quiet man, more interested in
action than talking about it and now he asked,
"Sir, can we just take a short look around the
fortress? It might be interesting to see what's
outside."

"Why not." Ivan frowned. "We'd better
make it snappy, but for God's sake skip the 'sir'

or I'll never live to make major!" Sep slapped
his forehead. He had just forgotten an important
rule of the game.

Ivan went on. "We'll tell Zoltan that Kish
and I'll be back in a few days before returning to
base. We're not coming back, but he'll just
decide something's happened to us. Let him
think so." Again Sep waited outside the house
with their gear, while the other two went in to
talk to Zoltan.

Vera had come home. She could have been
very beautiful—blue-black, thick gypsy hair
braided down her back, brown eyes shadowed
by long black lashes, creamy skin—but a ragged
scar cut across one cheek pulling one side of her
mouth. Following their look, Zoltan grimaced.
"The Nazis did that when she tried to stop them
from killing her mother. She was just a little
girl." His face was contorted with hate.

While Ivan asked a few questions, Kish
could hardly keep his eyes off Vera. This beautiful creature couldn't be an enemy. Her eyes met
his. He winked and a smile lifted one corner of
her mouth.

Although Vera was busying herself with pots
and pans, Ivan noticed she was listening to the
conversation and most certainly knew about her
grandfather's "connections". It was time to go.
Telling Zoltan they'd be back in a few days, the
SFs left the cottage. Outside, the coast was clear.
Ivan grinned. "Rather stay here, Ed?"

"Aw-w-w," Kish hid his expression as best
he could by rubbing his chin with both hands.
"She's one beautiful girl!"

Streets were wet, deserted, dark rivulets fill-
ing between cobblestones. The three SFs separated again, walking silently in the grass beside
a steep gravel footpath, which led up to the
ruins. Sep was some distance ahead on a side
path hoping to get a closer look at the fortress.

Hearing voices, Ivan and Kish inched over a
small ridge. They saw six Russian tanks in a

small clearing and soldiers smoking and talking
in low tones. They heard footsteps along the
path from the fortress and hunkered down in the
ditch. Two young Russian soldiers came into the
clearing and the guards turned over duty, still
smoking, heading up the path toward the
fortress. One of the new guards tipped back a
flask and then passed it to the other. They were
little more than boys and from snatches of conversation, Ukranians by their accent. "Zoltan's
granddaughter...beauty!...happen if he's lying!"

It was tempting to wait for the guards to get
thoroughly drunk and then remove essential
parts of the tanks, but Ivan decided it would only
delay their departure and possibly alert others in
the fortress—only a temporary gain anyway.

Meanwhile Sep heard the guards coming up
behind him on their way along the path to the
fortress. With a wall on one side and a cliff on
the other, there was no way to avoid them. Sep
groaned. He would have to try a bluff. As a last
resort he was sure he could pull his gun fast
enough, but he hoped it wouldn't be necessary.

Using his thickest Hungarian and pantomim-
ing, he hopped up and down in a weird imitation
of a Laurel and Hardy rerun. Giggling, he pointed to the town below.

The two young guards snickered and toyed
with their guns. "We ought to take this village
idiot to the Commandant," they said in Russian,
which Sep understood. He could see they were
more than a little drunk. That could have good or
bad consequences. His hair-trigger finger was
ready.

One of the guards finally said, "Oh, let him
go home to his mamma. Why bother with him."
They started up the path toward their waiting
rations, leaving Sep shambling down the path
toward town, maintaining his cover. He was cha-
grined by his own carelessness and never bur-
dened the other SFs with his story. It wouldn't
add anything to their information, but it worried

him the rest of his life.

The guards' voices faded, as Ivan and Kish crawled back along the ditch and saw Sep waiting for them. The three men slipped behind the shelter of the old fortress wall down to the Danube. Tied up to the dock they found a cluster of small skiffs and one boat that smelled powerfully of fish but would drift them down river well enough. "We shoulda brought some 4711 perfume!" whispered Sep, holding his nose. The oars were gone, but a pole lay on the riverbank that could be used to keep them away from shore. Though the current was slow, recent rains were strong enough to take them a good distance toward Budapest by daylight.

They untied the boat, left a packet of currency where the owner would find it, and pushed away from the bank. The current caught the boat and swung it downstream.

"Now this is more like it! Bring me a beer and my slippers!" Kish settled himself in the bottom. Sep said nothing. He was eating chocolate bars with a thoughtful expression on his face.

"Don't get too damned comfortable," warned Ivan. He stayed awake, watching the river, trying to see through the mist, remembering the guards talking about Vera. Was she the hold the Russians—or the AVO—had over Zoltan? It would be worth reporting if they made it back to Tölz. The old man had stayed out of trouble so far by playing both ends against the middle. No need to jump in the river to rescue damsels in distress, especially if they were the enemy. We've got a mission with enough problems already!

He wondered if Kate was in bed, reading a good book, maybe listening to music. Does Durwood miss me? Probably not, damn dog! There was another thought in his mind, but he didn't allow it to come to the surface. It had nothing whatever to do with the dog.

As the night wore on, Sep awoke and Ivan
took a turn in the bottom of the boat, saving himself for the day ahead. Once, Sep heard the soft
ripple of another small boat passing close to
theirs, oars almost silently dividing the water.
But the mist was thicker now and he could see
nothing. He poled along the shore away from the
sound until the current caught their boat again.

As the eastern sky began to lighten, the mist
raveled, moving thinly with them now, skim-
ming the surface. The boat was hidden and the
men sitting in it seemed to be riding on streamers of cloud. The current had taken them more
than halfway to Budapest, landing them in a
cove by Szentendrei Island just at daybreak.
They still had 20 kilometers to go.

"We lost our oars," they shouted to a group
of farmers on the river path with carts and horse-
drawn wagons filled with vegetables and crates
of chickens.

"Come join us," the peasants called back.
"We're on the way to take food to our families in
Budapest. There's going to be big trouble!" Sep
climbed into a wagon loaded with potatoes and
cabbages. Ivan found himself sitting on a crate
of geese, which he knew immediately was a mistake. He hopped down to walk with Kish along-
side one of the horses. When time came for a
rest stop, they told the farmers they were looking for brothers working in a locomotive factory
in Budapest.

CHAPTER THREE

In Flint Kaserne, Special Forces American Base on the outskirts of Bad Tölz, the Hungarian crisis was on everybody's mind, and Headquarters Company hovered between hope and despair. They knew how many expensive bottles of cognac it cost to soothe the Austrians when a new lieutenant had wandered by mistake over the border into neutral Austria taking his men with him. If the three members of their A-Team were discovered in either Austria or Hungary, it would be a catastrophe of international proportions. Headquarters would take the blame for getting their wires crossed, sending only part of the team. Worse, the official word to stay out of Hungary had been lost under a pile of papers. When it was found, Ivan, Sep and Kish were already on their way. Those responsible tried not to dwell on it, but were unable to think of anything else. Even their home lives were affected.

Lil, one of the wives, took her husband's odd behavior seriously and asked him point blank, "What on earth's the matter with you?" The first time she asked, Joe looked vacant and didn't answer. The second time, he considered and finally said, "We used to have an apple tree on the farm when I was a kid," adding, to her amazement, "Wanna go skiing some weekend in Austria?"

She thought of consulting the chaplain or the post doctor about her husband's condition, but decided to wait when her friend, Marge, another Headquarters Company wife, confided that her husband Bill was also acting strangely. "Something's going on," they agreed.

In case she had missed some alarming development, Lil read The *Stars and Stripes* from front to back every day. Now her glasses slid down on her nose and she pushed them up. "Do you think it's the trouble in Hungary?"

"Naw," said Marge. "More likely they're up for court martial. It's got to be something awful!"

Lil's jaw dropped. She hadn't thought of that. Hoping for the best, and without each other's knowledge, that night they both prepared a special dinner with steak, expensive wine and chocolate cake for dessert. Their husbands didn't seem to have much appetite.

Before Halloween, The Stars and Stripes was full of headlines about the Hungarian uprising. Two lieutenants, Jim Devorian and Hunk Bradford, stopped by Kate's quarters for a few minutes, which stretched into hours after they took their jump boots off and started on a bottle of scotch. They seemed subdued, not their usual wisecracking selves. Finally Kate broke one of their silences. "What do you think will happen in Hungary?"

"Too Goddamn much." Hunk looked gloomy. Devorian nodded.

"How come you're so pessimistic? Look what they've done," persisted Kate.

"Oh yeah! Look what they've done!" mimicked Devorian. He laughed to soften the sarcasm. "You don't think the Russians are going to let those little pipsqueaks thumb their noses at 'em, do ya? Not in a million years!"

Kate looked at Devorian in amazement. He was a dear friend like Ivan, but unlike Ivan, he never played games with her. What he said was what he meant. Now his laughter was forced.

Kate felt she was getting in over her head. "Well," she said slowly, "surely our country won't stand by and let Hungary go down the drain like the other satellites. This can't go on forever."

Hunk sat up from the floor where he was sprawled. "The Commies have the bomb." The words hung heavy in the air, menacing as a distant drum roll. "Do you listen to Radio Free Europe?" Then in a lighter tone, "Never mind,

Doll. It'll all come out in the wash." As the door closed after them, Kate remembered Charlie.

A week went by and Kate ran out of dog food. In the commissary she met Dave and Helen at the checkout counter. "Want some help with that bag?" Dave offered, taking the dog food off the counter while she paid the cashier.

"When is Ivan coming back, Dave?" she asked. "I love his dog but—."

"I dunno, kid. Don't worry. He'll be back."

"Where in heck is he? Living it up in Berlin?" asked Kate.

"Dunno, kid," Dave said again. He put the sack in her car and went back for the rest of the groceries.

Helen shrugged and rolled her eyes heavenward. "Full of information, isn't he!"

Kate waved at Helen and drove out of the commissary parking lot and into the military quadrangle. It was time for the mail truck from Munich, but rather than wait for the mail to be sorted, she parked in front of the snack bar and went in for a cup of coffee and maybe a doughnut. Looking at all that food in the commissary had made her hungry. Once inside, she decided to forget the doughnut, and carried her cup to a back corner table.

The coffee was too hot to drink. While it cooled, she looked around the snack bar. Over a scattering of customers she saw Jim Devorian come in the door. He caught her eye and aimed for her table, sliding his tall frame into the chair across from her. "Hello darlin'. How about sharing a jelly doughnut with me? Or are you waiting for someone?"

"I'm waiting just for you. Who else would know I'm dying for a doughnut?"

Jim looked happy and went off, digging in his pocket for cash. He came back with six jelly doughnuts and another cup of coffee.

"Thanks, Jim." She took a generous bite." You're my kind of fella."

Jim tested his coffee and set the cup down on his tray. "You're my kind of girl too, even with a mouthful of jelly." His lopsided grin faded. "'Fraid after I polish off this one, I've got a rendezvous with the Colonel. Damn it. I'd rather stay here with my favorite schoolteacher. You OK?"

"Fine." She hid her disappointment. "Except Ivan's dog is eating me out of house and home. Where is Ivan, or am I not supposed to know?"

"I dunno. He'll turn up soon enough." Devorian took another swallow of his coffee and stood up, rubbing his forehead as if to iron out a wrinkle. "See you soon, girl."

"Surely they won't send you guys out in the woods on Sunday. Come on over tomorrow and bring Hunk."

"Don't know yet, kid." He walked off, shaking his head. At the door he looked back at Kate as though he wanted to say something more. She wondered what he had forgotten. Kate looked down at four remaining doughnuts, wishing she and Devorian could have talked longer. Commanders always thought they owned the men, even on weekends.

While she lingered over another cup of coffee, she began to think about the first time she met Dave and Helen. Newly arrived from various tours of duty, they had wandered into one of her weekend gatherings. Helen hugged and kissed all those she didn't know as well as those she did know. Dave saw several old buddies, and they exchanged back whacks and obscene greetings. For a few minutes bedlam reigned supreme. Then Dave and Helen settled down comfortably on the living room floor.

"May we come in?" asked Helen with a roguish grin. "You must be Kate," adding with her hands in praying position, "Don't you have any strong drink in the house?" Kate had thought they were either crazy or drunk even by Saturday night standards.

Helen had a curly blond mop of hair that flew in all directions when she was excited, which was most of the time, and a raucous, infectious laugh. Drinking made her talkative. In contrast, her husband Dave became very quiet. Everyone agreed they were a perfectly matched couple although she was a bit taller than Dave's 5 feet 9 inches. If anyone alluded to this fact, however remotely, she would snarl, "I'll deck the next twit that asks if I played basketball in high school!" Kate laughed to herself. Helen's bark was worse than her bite. She had a heart of gold.

Kate finished her coffee and went down the hall to the mailroom. Sep's wife, Marie, was in line ahead of her. She turned and took Kate's hand. "Danny loves you to pieces. He's always talking about you, telling us what you said in class, how it's important to be kind to animals, read lots of books, and...more than you can imagine."

Kate smiled at Marie. "Danny's a good boy. You and Sgt. Sepeshy have done a great job of parenting."

"Thanks," Marie said. "We try. Sep is away right now. Danny misses his father so much when he's out on maneuvers." The line moved forward and Kate reached for her handout. There were only a couple of envelopes, nothing worth waiting for. She went back to the snack bar and bought a newspaper.

The news reported more conflicting and disturbing events—sporadic fighting in Budapest and Russian tank movements around the city. Durwood was acting strange, prowling around from room to room in her quarters and awakening her sometimes at night with a low mournful howl that made her hair prickle. They were both waiting. In fact the whole world was waiting. What happened and what did not happen changed the world for decades.

It was October 23rd. After entering the outskirts of Budapest, Ivan, Sep and Kish spent the
rest of the day establishing a new meeting place.
A cautious recon determined that a signal was
missing at the prearranged place to tell them the
rest of their team had arrived. It meant only one
thing. They weren't coming.

Not wanting to use any of Zoltan's contacts,
the three men moved into the central part of
Budapest. They blended into a large crowd of
university students and other people in front of
the Parliament Building. As darkness came the
crowd grew, and moved on to Radio Budapest.
AVO secret police guards, fearful of the huge
gathering and the explosive situation, their guns
pointed at the crowd, surrounded it.

Sep struck up a conversation with a
Hungarian journalist who was standing in the
crowd with his wife and teenage son. "This is
too dangerous for them," the journalist said,
pointing to his wife and son. "I can't persuade
them to go home. I should be here as a witness
for the truth, but they won't go home without
me."

"I'm from the country," said Sep. "Can you
tell me what you think will happen? I'm sure, as
a newspaper man, you know a lot more about it
than I do."

The journalist frowned. "Nobody knows
what will happen. I do know, if the Russians
come and we don't have help from the United
Nations and yes, America, we're finished. There
will be death in the streets and all over our land."

Sep was about to reply, but shouts from the
crowd and rising excitement created a rumble
like a storm brewing. Tear gas was thrown from
upper windows of the building. Beacons on the
roof lit the upturned faces of the people below.
The AVOs guarding the building panicked and
fired shots into the crowd.

When Sep turned, the writer was still standing, but blood was pouring from a hole in his

forehead. He was dead, held upright by the densely packed sea of people. They all surged back, almost trampling the man's wife and teenage son who were screaming, their voices lost in the uproar. Tear gas bombs were again thrown from the interior of the building and exploded, creating pandemonium and a rush toward Museum Park.

Ivan and Kish were close to Sep. Grabbing the woman and boy; they fought their way out of the crowd, while Sep managed to extricate the journalist's body. The woman was still screaming and sobbing until Ivan held his hand over her mouth. "Where do you live?" he asked gently but firmly. "We can't leave you here! Tell us and we'll find somebody to help you."

The woman was too shocked and terrified to talk, but already the boy was taking the place of his father, "Three streets over, the last apartment house on the right." He dug his fists into his eyes, gulping down his sobs.

Sep followed, carrying the journalist's body. There was a fountain in the courtyard of the apartment house and he washed as much of the blood as he could off the body and himself before going up the stairs to the second floor apartment where the family lived. The whole building seemed empty, but finally Kish found an apartment on the same floor where three frightened neighbor women huddled. News of the tragedy made them forget their own fear and they went to help their newly widowed friend and her son.

"If we can, we'll come back tomorrow," Ivan promised, and the SFs left the apartment house in the direction of Radio Budapest, keeping apart. From the shadow of a building across the street, they saw the area was still full of people. Most of the dead had been removed but some bodies had been dragged to the side and left. Charred remains of newspapers set afire by the insurgents littered the street and tear gas lingered in the air, stinging their eyes even at a distance. Blood stained the pavement.

As the SFs arrived there was an eerie silence. Even the air was still, as if the people in the square were holding their breath. Then someone shouted, "The Csepel men are coming!" There was a roar. Truckloads of workmen from the industrial east side of the city came to join the crowd. They had brought guns and ammunition. After setting up machine guns on the trucks, they shot out the beacon lights, and then aimed at the AVOs who had not yet retreated inside the building.

"Nothing to do here in this hell hole," said Ivan. "Better we miss some shut-eye and see if we can find out what the Russians are up to. Somehow I have this feeling the police and the soldiers in Kilián Barracks are going to be joining the fighters in droves. Not that it'll make any difference! We'll separate and throw our net as far as possible. With only three of us, Goddamn it! You go that way," motioning to Sep, "Kish, in that direction, and I'll take the east side. See you at the meeting place at 0430 hrs. For chrissake, be on time! I don't want to go looking for you!"

"Should we separate?" Kish wavered, remembering the rules.

"Right you are, ol' buddy!" Ivan gave him an approving nod. "But this time, if we want to know what's going on, we'll have to cover territory. For God's sake, let's stay out of trouble. Just observe. That's what we're doing, Goddamn it, observing. Now, sorry for the speech. Time to move out!"

During the hours of darkness they verified reports circulating around the city that Russian tanks were arriving from outside the suburbs. By morning they would be guarding bridges and strategic buildings all over Budapest. It was a night when almost no one slept. Stalin's statue was pulled down and spit upon; bookstores were demolished, their propaganda burned in the street; and gunfire marked scattered areas where death claimed many on both sides. When possible, along with the Red Cross and local medical teams, Ivan and the other two SFs helped take care of the wounded. They didn't stop for the dead.

By the middle of the morning, the battle for Budapest had begun in earnest. Fighter jets roared low over the city. Some women and children went out to stand in line for bread, in defiance of a declaration of martial law. Caught in crossfire or purposely shot by the secret police, civilians and Red Cross workers perished while they waited or tried to drag wounded people to safety. Lime was dusted on some of the unclaimed dead. October 24th dragged on; the stench of death and the acrid smell of burnt metal hung over the city.

Ivan was near Kilián Barracks where Hungarian soldiers without exception had turned overnight from Communists into rebels. They wanted only to drive the Russians out of their country and rid Hungary of the hated AVO secret police, who had tortured and killed their countrymen without mercy. Ironically these same soldiers had been trained by the Russians themselves to wage war with any weapons at hand and this they proceeded to do.

Few of the teenage volunteers who flocked to the barracks and the Corwin Cinema building across the street to join the soldiers had weapon training, but they had ingenuity, and Ivan found they learned fast. Between the withdrawal of Russian reconnaissance cars and the arrival of the first tank in Ulloi Street, he gathered one group of boys fourteen to eighteen years old. They had pried up paving stones and were aimlessly pitching them into the street. Three of them carried machine guns and ammunition they had taken from dead bodies, and one had made a gasoline bomb from a bottle.

"Here, fellows," Ivan told them. "This bomb

needs a longer fuse. When you throw it, wait 'til you see the side of the tank with the word 'petrol' marked on it and try to hit that exact spot. Don't stick around to see if it's going to go off! You can aim for the treads, but that may not stop the tank. If you're anywhere near a lone tank, stay low so its guns can't find you. But remember, other tanks can see you. Keep your eyes open and your wits about you!"

Ivan gave them some instruction on firing the machine guns and demonstrated how his own pistol worked. "Now, one last thing, men, never, never go anywhere alone. It's safer to stay with a group and you get more done. Now go report to the head man in charge of this building and do what he says. Good luck!"

As Ivan left the building to join Sep and Kish, he wondered how many of the boys would live through the coming night. Battle-wise from his own experience, he knew the adrenalin rush as the action begins and the aftermath as your friends fall around you. Just as he was thinking this, he saw a young boy no more than twelve, dash out from a side street, and Ivan heard Sep's voice shouting, "NO, not now!" The boy clambered up on a lone tank in the middle of Ulloi Street. A Mongol face peered out of the turret. The man seemed too surprised to aim and fire, or maybe he was out of ammunition. The face disappeared below the opening and the boy thrust his homemade bomb down the hatch.

The explosion threw the boy almost at Sep's feet. The last thing he saw was Sep's face blocking out the sky. There was only enough left of him to whisper, "When—will they—co—?" The boy was only a little older than his own son in Bad Tölz.

"Shit!" exclaimed Ivan. "That does it!" He raced along the outside wall of the building calling to Sep, who was holding the dead boy in his arms. AVOs and another Russian tank were converging on the square and a burst of gunfire ric-

ocheted off the walls. Kish appeared at the corner. Sep looked down at the dead boy cradled in
his arms, his face contorted. There were tears in
his eyes. "You're too young," he mumbled.
  Ivan controlled himself with an effort. The
other two showed signs of emotion that could
only put them in danger, and he forced his voice
to sound matter-of-fact. His tone was hard. "Lay
the boy here behind the wall. He's dead. We
can't change that. Head for the meeting place.
Now," he ordered as the other two lingered. Sep
found a Hungarian tricolor, and he took time to
put it on the boy's body where it turned a single
color—red. Then the three SFs left the body by
the building and quickly faded back into the
shadows of alleys and back streets to a vacant
house they had selected as a meeting place. It
was in a poor section of town surrounded by
shabby apartment buildings with broken shutters. Behind the house was a small neglected
garden with a few brown stalks left from a meager harvest. As they approached warily, the SFs
caught a glimpse of an old woman who had been
foraging in the weeds, shuffling away with a few
withered root vegetables bundled in her apron.
This area of the city appeared to be deserted.

CHAPTER FOUR

The old wooden walls of the SF's meeting place were partly fallen. The door was gone. A few rotten boards littered its sagging floor, and they picked their way carefully inside. It was still daylight, time to plan how to use the remaining hours before darkness.

"I need action!" Sep urged the other two.

Ivan looked him in the eye, showing no signs of sympathy. "We've got no damn business here. You know this rebel activity is only a delay. We have to get out, and it's going to take a lot of luck to make it over two borders." There was no need for discussion. The other two had to agree. "We'll get some down time at the journalist's place before we leave the city," Ivan continued. "Should be safe."

For the next several hours, staying a distance apart, they looked for new concentrations of Russian tanks and ammunition depots, testing the accuracy of rumors, gathering information that might prove valuable. Budapest had become a sea of tears filled with desperate, courageous people asking the same question, "When will they come?" as if their wishes would bring the world to help them. What they heard on Radio Free Europe sounded so much like promises.

Darkness came over the city, only lighted here and there by fires out of control. The SFs heard explosions in the distance as they kept in the shadows on their way to the journalist's home. Kish waited outside while the other two went in the entrance hall, climbed a flight of stairs, and knocked. The journalist's wife, pale, her eyes red-rimmed, recognized them and quickly invited them in. Janos, the son, was nowhere to be seen. They looked around the small room, bare of furniture except for a wooden cupboard, table, a padded corner bench by the stove and three chairs.

The woman could tell they were haggard

with fatigue and hungry from the way they
looked at the pot on the stove. She wasn't hungry but had prepared some food in case Janos
came home. "It's safe here," she said.

"Do you mind if our friend comes in and we
rest here awhile?" Ivan rubbed his stubble beard.

"Please." She pointed to a small bathroom.
"Help yourself. You are welcome." Kish joined
them. One at a time the men cleaned up, washed
their workmen shirts and hung them by the stove
to dry.

"What foreign news are you hearing on the
radio?" asked Ivan as they sat down to steaming
bowls of vegetable goulash heavily seasoned
with paprika and onions.

"I listened to Radio Free Europe before you
came," she answered. "It sounds like the UN and
maybe America will help us, but I don't know if
I understood it all. Too late to help my Imre.
Nothing will bring him back."

"Where is Janos?" Ivan asked, changing the
subject. He did not believe there was any hope
of foreign intervention, especially by the UN or
the United States. Their briefings had been quite
clear on that point.

"I don't know where my son is." Mrs.
Kovác's voice trembled, a shadow of tears in her
brown eyes. "He said he was going to join the
Freedom Fighters." She began to cry, wiping her
eyes on a corner of her apron, "He's so young
for all this horror. He had to bury his murdered
father in the courtyard last night. I made him
promise to be careful, but he said he was going
to kill all the AVOs and Communists he could
find."

They could offer her little comfort but Ivan
tried, cursing himself for bringing up the subject
of Janos. "He's a very brave and smart boy, Mrs.
Kovác. I'm sure he's going to come home to you
wearing the Hungarian tricolor. You can be
proud of him."

After they had eaten, she sent them to Janos'

room to sleep. Ivan told her they would leave in a few hours and would try not to disturb her. He had already decided on the best escape route, should they need it. He slept soundly until his eyes flew open at 0400 hrs, time to leave the city.

They put on all the clothing they had brought in their backpacks. The temperature was close to freezing. In their pockets were papers identifying them as farmers from a small town near Győr. Leaving half of their remaining forints on the kitchen table, the three men tiptoed out of the apartment and down the stairs.

"I feel guilty leaving these people. There aren't any cowards in the lot and the odds are damned awful!" Sep muttered, mostly to himself.

Ivan heard him. "Is there a better idea? Poor devils. It's a fuckin' shame! Now, let's hit the road before it's too late. We've got more than a hundred miles between the Austrian border and us. Keep your eyes peeled because it's going to be tricky." Ivan had never felt more frustrated. A fraction of his team had been sent into an impossible situation, a bullshit mess—doomed from the start.

During the last hours of darkness the three left the suburbs aiming west-northwest across Transdanubia toward the area north of Sopron where a small corner of Austria dipped into Hungary. They were going in the direction of a drainage canal, which flowed through marshland and under a very small and dilapidated wooden bridge. Beyond it was the Austrian border. The three men stayed away from main roads, walking day and night with only short stops for rest even when they reached the countryside. Now there seemed to be neither Russians nor police in the small towns and villages.

They caught a ride for a few miles on a freight train carrying a load of refugees from

Budapest. After two more days walking, they were within fifty kilometers from the Austrian border. Stopping at a small town cafe along the way, they began a conversation with some of the local farmers who were curious about three strangers in their midst. Ivan told them, "These are my two brothers, and we're on our way home in case the trouble spreads to Györ. What do you hear on the radio?"

A big bearded fellow spoke up. "The Russians are leaving Budapest and taking their tanks with them! The secret police are dead or running as fast as they can. That's what the freedom radio says. I heard it myself." He pounded the table in his glee.

Then the room was silent. Someone said, "Maybe—if help comes in time." The stove by their table gave out waves of warmth; the food was good as well as the beer warmed by a glass tube of hot water. Ivan began to feel relaxed and sleepy; his eyelids sagged and he had to slap the back of his head to stay awake. It was time to go.

In spite of the loss of uncounted men, women and children in the battle for their capital, for a few days, Hungarians were euphoric over their new freedom—foreign newspapers to read, stores open for business, political discussions on the street. This was the narrow window of opportunity during which Ivan, Kish, and Sep finally crossed the bridge. Soon after they went over, it became the crossing point for a mass migration of refugees out of Hungary. By that time police manned the guard tower with searchlights. Adding to the danger, the terrible cold and exhaustion made escape impossible for some of the refugees, especially children and old people. Even those who had almost reached the bridge were often shot or taken away to prison, where they were starved and tortured by the AVOS, their own people. It was the end of their short-lived dream of a free Hungary.

The three SFs headed for home base, but

they had only one reliable contact in Austria where they could replenish their supplies without relying on survival methods. Now some rough mountainous terrain lay between them and the German border. "Goddamn it," muttered Ivan. "Should I start a chorus of Onward Christian Soldiers or what?"

"Naw," said Kish, "just throw me a bottle of black label—or any color label."

They all groaned in unison and then Sep had an idea. "There's a small Hütte just beyond this ridge where I went hunting once. The owner lives in Innsbruck. The place is only used in the summer by an old woman who brings her cows to graze in the Alm and makes cheese there. She takes the cows home in October before the first big frost. She'll be gone by now." It was a long speech for Sep. A real roof over their heads would be good medicine, and he was almost home. He felt a glow of anticipation.

They reached a line of trees stunted by Alpine winds along the ridge and looked down a rocky slope to a small green meadow. There was the Hütte, its roof secured from winter storms by heavy stones. Shutters were closed on the two small windows they could see in the evening gloom. The sun was almost down and the air was colder. "She's gone," Sep said, and the three walked down the slope.

"If somebody's there, have we got a story?" Sep asked.

"Sure. Remember Lesson 1," answered Ivan. They didn't need Lesson 1. They saw nobody. It was easy to get in. That was Lesson 1 1/2. But the interior was not welcoming—a dirt floor with only a wooden corner bench and a table with two chairs. A narrow bed leaned against one wall. Sep's flashlight went out as he ventured into an extension of the room they had first entered. He stubbed his toe on something hard which, when he lit a match, turned out to be one of the flat slabs of an open stone hearth. A large

blackened copper kettle hung above it attached
to the low ceiling by a heavy iron chain. Beside
the hearth were a pile of kindling and an ax driv-
en into a tree stump. The room held nothing else
except two cheese presses and some splintered
shelves.

"Sep, you've really brought us to heaven,"
groaned Kish.

"At least, if it snows we won't have to build
a lean-to, and you can always sleep in a cheese
press," replied Sep. "Quit bitchin'. We're almost
home."

"The barracks ain't home. No way." Kish
ducked outside through the low door and came
back with thick chunks of wood, which had been
piled against the Hütte under its projecting roof.
Soon they had a fire going, and the clammy chill
went out of the room. They heated water for coffee, ate their last can of dried meat, and slept
soundly until dawn. That day, invigorated by the
nearness of home base, the three SFs made good
time, arriving in Flint Kaserne just after the flag
ceremony.

Joe and Bill in Headquarters Company
breathed a big sigh of relief when the three
showed up in the office, slapping them heartily
on the back and commenting sotto voce, "We
couldn't 've covered your ass much longer. And
we don't want any damned after-action report.
Just say you were in the hospital in Never Never
Land with the plague."

The three were furious. "Who the hell sent
us out there?"

"We know. We know." was the glum answer
as the accused found urgent business in the
direction of the rigger shed. Debriefing could
wait until later; when they could figure out if
anybody wanted to hear about it.

"Goddamn it! You owe us a night at the bar
and that's just for starters!" Ivan shouted after
them.

That evening Durwood began barking and

jumping on Kate's door. Ivan was back. Kate opened the door and waited while the dog and man hugged each other. A warm feeling came over Ivan. It wasn't just the dog. Kate's apartment felt like home. That's what it was. He took a deep breath and said, "Hello, girl," settling himself on the sofa. "Got anything to drink?" The dog lay down at Ivan's feet, rubbing his muzzle against his owner's feet. Kate brought two drinks, not asking any questions. They talked about nothing in particular, were sometimes silent, and in the middle of one of his favorite recordings, he went to sleep with an arm over his eyes. Kate added a blanket and went off to bed, setting her alarm to get him out before the Kaserne came to life in the morning.

She lay awake for a while considering their relationship. He was taking her for granted and making her apartment a home away from home. She allowed herself some self-pity. The next thing she knew, the alarm went off and when she went to awaken Ivan, he and the dog were gone—the blanket dumped in a wad on the floor. "Son-of-a-bitch!" she exclaimed loudly, wondering why she was so exasperated. "For a smart guy, he's really dumb! Hell no! I'm the one who's the dummy!" This was unsettling so she put on the coffee pot. In her haste she knocked her favorite mug from Venice off the table, and it landed on the floor, smashing into a thousand pieces. "Damn! Damn! Damn!" She grabbed a broom.

CHAPTER FIVE

Lieutenant Ron "The Con" Ariste was always looking for an easy mark, and Cassie, a secretary at Flint Kaserne Base Headquarters, was the perfect victim—plain, vulnerable, and afraid life was passing her by. Not that he meant any harm. In fact, he thought he was doing her a favor when he invited her along on a non-existent mission in the three-mile buffer zone between Germany and Czechoslavakia. His lead was textbook perfect—drinks at Freddie's Bar, slow dancing at Maximilian's, sitting in a parked car beside Tegernsee, and a long kiss as rain dripped down from the trees and mist rose from the lake, closing them in a thick white blanket of fog.

Ron was almost too short for the Special Forces. He had the rich, compelling voice of a good actor, which had something to do with the shape of his nose. According to his version, he was in the midst of divorcing a wife and four children in the States. But none of this prevented him from persuading a WAC in Stuttgart that he was going to marry her. For him, life was a big joke, devil take the hindmost. His affairs were as tangled as the fire escapes in the Park Hotel Officer's Club. The Park Hotel was gone, but its legends lived on. Some of the stories were about Ron.

The scene in the car parked by the shore of Tegernsee was well written. "I know a place that's almost as beautiful as this. There's a castle few people ever see because it's in Lauenstein in the forbidden area between Germany and Czechoslavakia. I have to go there on a mission very soon. Wish I could take you."

"Oh, I wish you could! It sounds exciting!" Cassie saw adventure just beyond her grasp.

"Hey, wait a minute! Why couldn't you go? It'll be a weekend. We won't tell anybody and nobody'll ever know. How about it?"

"Won't it be dangerous?" Cassie looked a little nervous. She began to wonder just what was involved—too much adventure?

"No, no. Anyway, I'll be with you. Nothing to worry about." Not entirely reassured, Cassie said she'd think about it. A small voice was talking to her—"You know how he always swings you out at the end of a dance, off balance."

Women hardly ever listen to small voices, so when Ron called and said official orders were cut and there would be no trouble getting past the MPs into the buffer zone, she packed a small bag and off they went in an old Volkswagon "bug" with German plates. He showed her how the "mox nix" turn signals worked like a lever and kept her laughing all the way to Bayreuth with stories about life in the military—the horror of a family moving out of quarters charged for a lost navy boat instead of a gravy boat. Other nonsense followed, told in Ron's most charming manner.

Beyond Bayreuth the road became smaller and they passed only a few small houses clustered around crossroads. The MP station at the edge of the buffer zone did not challenge their German car, and the road began to climb hills to the rim of a valley forested except for patches and outcroppings along the river.

Lauenstein was a few small old houses, a tiny kiosk, and the remains of a castle in dilapidated condition and a Gasthaus where Ron pulled up and parked the car. There seemed to be nobody there, but finally an old man appeared walking with a cane. "Zimmer frei?" asked Ron.

"Was?" The man cupped his ear. Ron repeated his question and the old man nodded "Yo," gesturing for them to follow him down a dark hallway.

"Zwei Zimmer!" Cassie said with determination, and the man went back to get a second key. It didn't look as though there was much excitement around Lauenstein. The room smelled of dust but the bed looked clean. Three windows overlooked the valley, and she saw a tower about a mile away just below the ridge.

Ron pulled a pair of binoculars out of his bag. "That's a Commie watchtower." When Cassie looked she thought she could see the top of a man in uniform inside the tower. She'd been afraid Kate would not approve of her adventure and told her she was going to spend the weekend with friends in Rothenburg, a ruse she already regretted. Nobody knew where she was.

There was time for a short walk around the village before the sun went down, and they went into the Gasthaus for supper. In the meantime a younger man, Johann, evidently the old man's son, was taking care of the place. They sat down at one of two long tables. He offered them a well worn, spotted menu, but only one dish was available in the kitchen—a stew of sausage, cabbage, carrots, and potatoes accompanied by hunks of dark bread. At Ron's request, Johann brought a carafe of local red wine, strong and good with the stew.

While they ate, Ron told her, "The border is a road along the riverbank. Men who work on opposite sides of the border cross every day without any interference. They drink beer together in a small Gasthaus down there every night. Really."

Much to her surprise, Ron left her with a light kiss at the door of her room saying, "Sleep tight, Babe."

She woke up in the middle of the night, confused and wondering what had awakened her. Then it came again—footsteps and a door closing softly. Actually Ron was just coming back from a frolic with a bar girl down by the river, but she had no way of knowing that. Moonlight was streaming in the window making patterns on the wooden floor. The valley spread below, a white sea of mist rising and hiding the lower slopes, but the outline of the watchtower was

still visible. A shiver went down her back. She
listened for a few seconds but heard no more
sounds, so she pulled the Federkissen over her
head and dozed off to sleep.

At 9:00 the sun woke her up. Dressing in a
hurry, she knocked on Ron's door. He sounded
sleepy. "I'll meet you for breakfast in half an
hour." She sat down at a table and opened a
German newspaper two days old. Ron sauntered
in fifteen minutes late looking tired. Coffee
came in two big steaming mugs followed by
more of the dark bread, a crock of butter and
marmalade. Ron's spirits seemed to improve.
"Did I tell you there's supposed to be a ghost in
this Gasthaus? Way back when it was the gate-
house for Burg Lauenstein. The lady of the castle fell in love with the gatekeeper, and her husband killed them both with his sword."

"Maybe I heard the ghost last night."

"I guess so." He laughed. "Woo-o-o——-w-o-
O!" flapping his arms like a crow. "Let's go look
at the castle." He pulled her away from the table.
Johann said his boy would take them through.
He knew where the floors were unsafe to walk
on.

The tour didn't take long. Evidently they
were the first visitors in a long time to disturb
layers of dust collected during years of neglect.
Nothing remained of the towers but part of the
outer structure, and the small dark rooms were
empty except for a couple of old carpenter's
benches and a dagger that looked like a stage
prop for the story of the murders. At the end Ron
gave the boy a couple of deutsche Marks. He
dashed off in the direction of the kiosk grinning
from ear to ear. They followed at a more leisure-
ly pace. There was no hurry and nothing much to
buy there, but Ron bought her the only two wine
glasses on display. They were decorated with a
gold leaf picture of the castle as it was supposed
to look and didn't.

Ron yawned saying he was tired and needed

some shut-eye. He'd be okay by 5:30. "Just
don't go out of town," he called over his shoulder and headed back to the hotel. Cassie was disgusted with herself for coming and with Ron for
leaving her in this boring, Godforsaken place.
What to do? Nobody seemed to be around in the
paths and lanes of the village, and she began to
get a creepy feeling. The kiosk was closed now,
and in the Gasthaus Johann and the boy had disappeared. She found herself mumbling, "No one
was stirring, not even a mouse," jumping at the
sound of her own voice, half expecting a mouse
to skitter out of the kitchen.

The key was hanging outside her room. She
ran inside and double locked the door. Dark
clouds were gathering in the east, and the one
dim light bulb hung unshaded in the middle of
the room—impossible to read the book she had
brought. Her anger rose in waves until she was
stiff with fury. What a fool I am! Why, why did
I come? How could I get myself in such a mess!
Time dragged on and a pinpoint of light showed
in the watchtower. Suddenly rain came in sheets,
wind-driven, lashing and beating on the windows, reaching in.

The room was cold and she curled up under
the featherbed. Something was flapping outside
her door. She heard rising and falling sounds,
"Woo-o-oo-O-wO-O! Before she could scream
she heard a muffled laugh and Ron's voice, "It's
me. Open the door!"

She opened it a crack scowling, "It's not
funny you—"

He was standing there wrapped in his own
featherbed, waving a bottle of wine and trilling
"Woo-oo-Oo!" between laughs. It was too
much. They collapsed on the bed in helpless
laughter, hopelessly entangled in two feath-
erbeds. Ron found her in the middle, half suffo-
cated, struggling against his mouth pressed hard
on hers. She stopped thinking, giving herself up
completely to this new pleasure that far exceed-

ed her dreams. Ron felt a rush of power. His face
became the mask of a satyr, while he mentally
chalked up number 29. He smiled again, remembering the wine.

It was part of Ron's genius that his victims
seldom blamed him for their misfortunes. He
woke Cassie at 0430 hrs. "Pack your bag, girl.
We're leaving in five minutes!" On the way
home, while she was calling herself a stupid
idiot, Ron was mostly silent, not bothering about
his companion, thinking ahead to his next
adventure.

"He doesn't even remember I'm along!" she
thought miserably. "I'm such a fool!" The ride
back seemed very long. Ron drove through the
Kaserne gate faster than was allowed.

The MP at the gate saw the girl in the car and
decided not to pull him over. They saluted and
the car whizzed on into the quadrangle. The MP
frowned. "What's the lieutenant up to now?
These officers! Next time he won't get off so
easy. Thinks he owns the damn place."

Ron stopped in front of House 71 and smiled
pleasantly, "Goodbye, kid. See ya."

Cassie mumbled "Bye." She could hear his
car going up the hill as she carried her overnight
bag up the sidewalk and in the door. She ran up
the stairs wishing she could hide in a dark clos-
et and never come out. Inside her apartment,
Cassie dumped her clothes on the floor and
added more from her bag in a pile for the laun-
dry. Then she went into the shower, turning on
the water as hot as she could stand.

At work the following week, the major in
charge of the base noticed Cassie seemed preoc-
cupied and frequently asked him to repeat dicta-
tion. By Friday, he ran out of patience. "What's
the matter, Cassie? Have you had a death in the
family or what?"

She jumped. "No sir. I'll try to do better.
Really, I'm fine," and started to cry.

He gave up. "Go on home and take it easy

over the weekend. I'll see you Monday."

"Thank you, sir," she sniffled. Cassie wiped her eyes, put on her dark glasses, and hurried out of the office to the sanctuary of her apartment.

That Saturday there was an impromptu party at Kate's. Ron's WAC girl friend from Stuttgart was visiting him and he brought her along. When Cassie arrived at the door she heard Ron's rich laugh and caught a glimpse of the back of his head and his arm around the WAC. She was gazing at him adoringly. Cassie turned and fled before anyone saw her, and when Kate called her to come down, she said she had a bad headache, which was true. "Are we making too much noise down here? I'll make 'em tune it down! Or go someplace else—. Anything I can do for you, Cass?"

"No, no. Don't worry about the music. I can hardly hear it. I'll be fine." Cassie didn't sound just right, but Kate decided it would be better to let her sleep it off. Next day the word went around that the WAC was going on leave in the States to buy her trousseau for the wedding.

Nothing more was ever heard about the wedding, and before Christmas Ron left the Army, some said by request. A year later Kate heard he was broadcasting news from a local radio station in Alaska. His buddies thought it likely that Ron's wife and four children were inventions of his fertile imagination. As for the WAC, neither Kate nor Cassie ever heard of her again, probably because she married someone in her hometown.

CHAPTER SIX

After Christmas, skiing was good at the Jägeralm so Ivan, his buddy Jim Devorian, Kate, and a few couples decided to go up to the Hütte for a weekend. Cassie had been looking down in the mouth, and Kate asked her to come along. "I don't really ski very well," Cassie objected.

"Bring a good book if you don't want to ski. It'll be fun, and it's beautiful up there in the mountains."

"The last time I took a book—" Cassie stopped.

"You'll like it," Kate promised.

"I guess so." Cassie looked doubtful.

It was Thursday night and Ivan stopped by Kate's on his way to the BOQ. "What about the dog while we're off skiing?" Kate asked. "You're not going to take him, are you?"

"Of course not. He likes Sep's family. They'll take care of him."

On an impulse, Kate suggested to Ivan that he bring Kish along to the Jägeralm. "Why?" asked Ivan. "He gets enough skiing when he's training."

"So do you." Kate was persistent. "He's one of your good buddies."

"Well, if I see him. Do you have some ulterior motive?"

"No-o. Don't you want him along? Is it because Ed's not an officer?"

He scowled at her. "What do you think I am? A complete ass? Okay, okay." He hoped Kate didn't have designs on Kish. He was at least a head shorter than she was!

Early Saturday morning Ivan picked up Kate who had Cassie in tow. They arrived at the foot of the lift just as the rest of their group disappeared over the first hill on the way up the mountain to the Hütte. "Grab your skis! Hurry up! Every man for himself!" Ivan was not waiting.

"Go on. Don't wait for us!" Kate called. She doubted that he even heard her. "Come on, Cassie. We'll damn well fend for ourselves!" She helped Cassie on the lift and followed behind her up the mountain.

When Ivan came up from a run down to Kreuth and saw Kish taking Cassie toward the baby slope, the light dawned. "Aha! I know what you're up to!"

"Who me?" Kate put on her goggles and headed for the advanced beginner slope.

That night the weather closed in. Nothing could be seen outside the Hütte except a whirl of white flakes. Gusts of wind rattled windows and howled down the chimney. "Should be good powder tomorrow," said Hans, fingering his zither. "Probably clear by late morning."

"Prost!" They drank to that and settled down to the warmth of candlelight, hearty Wienerbrot, Bier, and the music of Hans' zither accompanied by Franzl's guitar. Everything else outside the surrounding whiteness seemed faraway and unimportant. The faces of the people in the room took on the rapt, drowsy look of children listening to a favorite bedtime story.

It was still early in the evening when they climbed the ladder to the lager storeroom. Ivan chose the mattress next to Kate's and rolled out his sleeping bag, reaching over to grab her hand. "Come closer, dream girl. These mattresses are too far apart or we could bundle! With all these clothes on we could do a very authentic job of it."

"I'll bet several hundred guys have said the same thing in this exact same place—but," she added rather hopefully, "it's not a bad idea." Ivan didn't answer. A variety of snores came from all directions.

"Damn," Kate exclaimed, intending to wake him up. He did not hear her. Nobody heard her. They were all asleep. Kate snuggled down in her sleeping bag and shut her eyes. She dreamed that

Ivan was holding her close in his arms. The odd part was, she knew, without waking up, it was nothing but a dream.

In the morning Kate opened her eyes to find the lager empty. Through the ladder opening rose the fragrance of strong coffee. Most of the others were finished with breakfast by the time she climbed down, but Cassie was still there. The sun came out, and they could see the Hirschhorn, a white giant in a tumble of mountains covered with dazzling diamonds. The snowpack was powder perfect. The expert skiers had hurried out, taking off down the slope, leaving behind them a spume of dry flying snow that caught the sun in vanishing rainbows of color.

After his first run, Kish came back to the Hütte where Kate and Cassie were lingering over coffee. "Come on, Cassie. I'll show you some more stuff. You too, Miss O'Brien, if you want to, but you don't need any lessons."

"No thanks, Kish, and call me Kate. I'm going to wait awhile." She had another cup of coffee, put on a liberal coat of sun lotion, and stretched out in a folding chair on the terrace, lazy as a turtle, absorbing the mountains, the bright cold air and warm sunshine, wanting the feeling to last forever.

By lunchtime she had roused herself to take a couple of runs with Jim Devorian and, halfway down the trail, a single spill. She found Cassie at the Hütte telling Kish she was dead tired and sending him off to the fast slope with the others. After he had gone, Cassie leaned on her skis, panting. "Whew! That was some fun but hard work! I'm exhausted."

"You need a cup of strong brew," said Kate, seeing Cassie's plain face pink and glowing with pleasure. She looked really pretty!

"Ed is so nice," Cassie smiled,"—never gets impatient or tries to hurry you. Anyway, he shouldn't have spent so much time with me instead of going with the good skiers."

"He must have wanted to," Kate told her. "He's got the whole afternoon for serious skiing. They make trail designs, you know, where nobody's been since the fresh snow. Personally, I like a well-marked trail with no curlicues. C'mon. Let's take the lift down, and I'll treat you to something with whipped cream at the Konditerei."

They propped their skis in a snow bank and caught the lift as it started down the mountain. They both yawned and Kate called to Cassie in the chair ahead of her, "It's the fresh air." They were still yawning when they ordered coffee and lingered over flaky Apfelstrudel with whipped cream. Kate took pictures of Cassie and then they caught the lift back up to meet the others. The mountain peaks turned pale pink and faded to gray by the time they reached the Hütte. It was time to go home.

The crowd from Tölz trudged down to where their cars waited in a parking place by the lift. The cold was now bone-chilling in the early evening darkness. Kish asked Cassie to ride with him, and she beamed with pleasure. There was a full moon and snow conditions were right so Kate asked Ivan, "Why don't we take a sleigh ride from Kreuth on the logging trail down to Rottach. You can get somebody to drive your car down." "Damn! I'd rather ski along behind," growled Ivan. "I'd go if you could yodel. Gimme a break!" He snickered, "S'pose you're looking for one of those mountaintop experiences!"

"Well, I'll go by myself! Meet you in Rottach." Why was he such a joker? Sometimes she thought they sounded like an old married couple arguing about nothing.

Jim Devorian came along, put his skis in the sleigh and climbed in beside Kate. "Let's make it a troika."

Ivan snorted, "A troika is three horses, not three people, you dummy!"

"Okay, smartass!" Jim leaned back in his seat and winked at Kate. "Run ahead with the horses if you want to!"

"All right! ALL RIGHT! I'll go. Dave, wouldya mind taking my car down to Rottach?" Ivan threw him keys. "Helen can drive yours. Thanks ol' buddy." He climbed into the sleigh grumbling, "See how nice I am?" The driver draped a horse blanket over their knees, and the sleigh started down the narrow road through the forest, runners squeaking, and mountains black and frost-white in the moonlight. Ivan put his arm around her. "Snuggle up, kid. It's cold outside!"

"Isn't this great!" She was laughing. "I'm escorted by the two most handsome Green Berets in the 10th!"

"Yeah, yeah, Babe!" Then they were quiet, watching the black and silver forest slide by the sleigh. Disturbed by its passing, an occasional snow shower from heavy hanging branches slanted down, touching their faces.

"It wasn't so bad," Ivan admitted as he and Jim paid off the driver.

Kate chided, "You can't jump out of airplanes all the time." Jim grinned at her and climbed into the back seat of Ivan's car. On the way back to Tölz, they passed Cassie and Ed Kish who seemed to be driving rather slowly. Kate congratulated herself on being a good matchmaker. Cassie needed a nice man like Ed Kish. Ivan hadn't even noticed Cassie wasn't riding home with them.

Back at the door of Cassie's quarters in Flint Kaserne, Kish gazed at her, smiling. She wasn't a looker like Vera, but he'd never have to worry whether she was telling the truth. They were both exceptionally contented with each other.

Monday after school, Kate went up to Cassie's quarters expecting her to be excited about her new friend Kish. Instead Cassie's eyes were red-rimmed. She was crying. "What on earth's the matter?" Kate asked. "What's happened?"

"Sit down, please—please. I need to talk to you. Oh God, what am I going to do?" Cassie sobbed.

"How do I know? Sorry! Guess you're asking God, not me!" Kate was annoyed and her tone was sharper than she intended. "What are you bawling about? Talk to me!" If Kish could see her now—red nose, lanky hair—impossible hair.

Cassie was near hysteria, but she stopped crying and blew her nose. "Kate, I'm—I-I think I'm pregnant." Her voice wobbled and tears streaked down her face again.

Kate was silent for a full minute. What bad timing—just as Cassie was about to have a real romance. She ventured, "Who was it? Do you want to tell me?"

"It was that damn trip to Lauenstein. Why on earth did I go?"

"Lauenstein? What are you talking about?" And then the whole story came out. Kate sat, unbelieving. Everybody knew Ron was a con artist, and where in heaven's name was he now? And if he knew, he'd probably get lost in Timbuktu. That devil would go after poor naive Cassie! She said, "Maybe it isn't true. Maybe you're not. Why don't you go to a German doctor downtown tomorrow? We'll think about it after that. Now try to pull yourself together, take an aspirin. Put some ice on your eyes."

"What if Kish calls?"

"You'll just have to put up a brave front and tell him you're resting from all that unaccustomed exercise. Don't let him see you looking like a fright!" Cassie had an irritating habit of tweaking her nose two or three times, then working over that portion of her face like a baker manipulating bread dough. Repetition of her nervous tic had added to the disaster even more than her tears. Kate thought "fright" wasn't really the right word for her puffy appearance, but in the circumstances it was no time to worry about details.

The next day Cassie's news was as bad as they expected, and she was distraught to the point of talking suicide. Thinking about it, Kate was worried about being the only one who knew. Cassie is such a helpless girl, and it's none of my business. Why do I get mixed up in other people's affairs? I should be having some of my own!

Ivan stopped by Kate's apartment a day later, and the conversation gave her an opportunity. "What do you Green Berets do when you get a girl in trouble?"

"Run like hell," he said, grinning at her. "Anyway, we don't get 'em in trouble; they get US in—" interrupting himself, "Hey! Wait a minute. You're not—!"

"Of course I am, —expecting triplets." She gave him a disgusted look, which sent him off into loud guffaws.

He got serious. "I'd make an honest woman out of you." She thought he probably would.

During the next days, Kate spent as much time with Cassie as possible, mostly listening. Sometimes her wild statements prompted Kate to say as firmly as she could, "You don't have to decide anything now. Wait and think it over when you aren't so excited. You have time. Promise me!"

Then Cassie would calm down but was apt to list the possibilities—suicide, abortion, marry somebody, interjecting, "I know Kish won't want me now!"

Kate wondered if their friendship had already progressed so far in one short weekend. "How do you know that?" she asked. Are you sure you want to tell him? And for God's sake, stop saying the word 'suicide'!" Then Kate would clamp her mouth shut, and go on listening until they were both exhausted.

The next Friday night Kate knocked on
Cassie's door to invite her to dinner. There was
no answer. She panicked and ran downstairs to
get Cassie's key. "Why didn't I tell somebody?
Get some help?" Her heart was thudding. She
felt sick. At the top of the stairs she stopped,
took a deep breath and braced herself for the
worst.

At first the key refused to go in the lock until
she realized she was trying to force it in upside
down. She fumbled and dropped it on the floor.
Groaning and swearing, Kate finally got the
door open and looked down the long hallway—
only silence, which did not reassure her. She
called Cassie's name. It came out a squeak. Her
mind worked furiously. Whom should she call
for help—the dispensary, the chaplain? Her eye
caught an envelope on the hall table. It was
addressed to her. A suicide note? She tore it
open.

"I've gone to a place in Austria I heard
about. Don't worry. Probably I'll be back by
Monday night. If not, please call the office and
tell them I'm still sick. Thanks for listening. I
haven't told anybody else. See you. Cass."

Kate sat down in a chair until she could stop
shaking.

Cassie came back late Monday looking pale
and listless and didn't go to work until
Wednesday. She and Kate never mentioned the
matter, and Kish had no inkling Cassie was hiding something from him that could ruin everything.

CHAPTER SEVEN

It was a hard winter even for Upper Bavaria. Kate's third graders were more lively than usual, there were long parent-teacher conferences; snowplows cleared the roads and the smell of wet boots filled classrooms. By the time the third graders put on their snowsuits and found their boots for recess, it was time to come in and take them off. On maneuvers the Green Berets slept in most of the warm barns and haystacks in their training area.

Two new teachers had been transferred to Bad Tölz in midwinter. They were having dinner at the Officer's Club with Kate. "What's the principal like? Is she a witch?"

Kate smiled. "Do I look downtrodden?"

They laughed and turned their attention to the men gathered around the bar. "Are those Green Berets? Are they really wild? They look pretty normal except—they do look kind of cocky—or maybe just sure of themselves."

Pretty good for beginners, Kate said to herself but answered aloud, "I'm not convinced there's a category that fits any two SFs. They don't wear green berets all the time."

The dessert special was finished, and the newcomers were glancing sideways at the men around the bar, who were sizing them up at the same time. Two officers strolled over to their table. Kate introduced them and left, saying she had some work to do. "I'll pick you up for school tomorrow. We've got a meeting at 9:00."

"Can we come too?" the SFs called after her. She waved goodbye, thinking they looked younger every year—not like the old crowd.

But some of the old crowd were returning, among them Jim Devorian and Hunk Bradford. Hunk's buddies nicknamed Angela Reilly, the eighth grade teacher, Angel, because she was rumored to be a virgin, but Hunk was serious when he called her Angel.

A natural strawberry blonde whose eighth grade worshiped her individually and collectively, Angela was used to being the center of attention. The only girl in a family with seven sons, she was petted and protected from life's evil from the day she was born. Her eighth graders considered it an honor to trade and correct each other's papers so she wouldn't have to grade them after school. They also cleaned the blackboards thoroughly and saw to it that wastepaper landed in the wastebasket instead of being used as missiles. She lived life on a pedestal. Consequently, when she went to confession on Sundays, she had little to confess except that one of her beaus had tried to kiss her. The kiss had landed on her forehead because of prompt action on her part, and no Hail Marys were required.

Angela accepted Hunk's adoration as no more than her due. It was pleasant to have a handsome and devoted beau available for parties and official functions. She realized it was often customary to marry after these preliminaries but gave the idea little thought as long as she was having a good time.

While Hunk's courtship continued, a suitor from the States came to visit her in Bad Tölz. Arthur was a talented artist and he longed to paint her picture now that he was famous in their home town. When he arrived at her door bearing an armload of pink roses, she was flattered to the point of promising to go with him to Garmisch for the weekend, so he could depict her against a background of Alps with the Zugspitze prominently placed just behind her head.

When she heard about it, Kate concealed her astonishment. "Wonderful! Be sure to see the ice show at the Casa Carioca. Arthur will love it!"

"Yes, we might have time for that, but Art may paint in the evening too. He's very serious about his work and wants this to be his masterpiece."

"Really? Will he give it to you?"

"Could be." Angela smiled smugly looking her most beautiful.

Saturday evening, Kate heard a door slam in Angela's apartment next door, and when more loud noises followed, decided to investigate. Angela cracked the door, mumbling, "Oh, it's you."

"Who else?" Kate stepped back. "Shall I go away?" Angela's face was a grimace, furious. Kate turned to go but Angela stopped her.

"I've nearly killed somebody."

"Wha-a-a-t?" Kate stepped inside and sat down in the nearest chair. This was going to take awhile. She hoped it wasn't anything like Cassie's problem. What next!

Angela wailed, "I wish I had. I trusted him! I thought he was my frien-n-d!"

"You can't mean what's his name—Arthur."

"Yes I do mean—oh, I'll never ever say his name again." Kate waited. "He made a pass at me. He's an animal!"

"Well," Kate tried to sound reasonable, "you did go to Garmisch with him for the weekend. Where is he?"

"I don't care where he is. He tried to stop me from driving home. I almost ran over him."

"You mean you left him there without transportation, and you tried to run over him?"

Angela looked at her in disgust. "What would you do if a man wanted to paint you without any clothes on?"

"Well, let's see. I wouldn't try to murder him. It might turn out to be interesting." Kate went home leaving Angela speechless with horror.

An hour later Angela rode off with Hunk in his car. She looked as perfect as usual.

After a month, when Angela finally said yes to the adoring Lieutenant Henry "Hunk" Bradford's proposal of marriage, it called for some form of celebration. Jim Devorian was appointed to the Decoration Committee and spray-painted the ceiling of the Bachelor Officers Quarters lobby with their names in a large red heart. It created the necessary festive atmosphere. Hunk's buddies attended with mixed emotions since, without exception, they believed he was making a terrible mistake, and not because Angel might or might not be a virgin. Hunk himself, a big paratrooper with a quarterback physique and a happy-go-lucky little boy at heart, found out they were right, but that was some time later.

The night of the party he was in an expansive mood and blissfully unaware of what the stars had in store for him. Tanked up with champagne, he called for quiet, which was difficult to achieve amid a dozen simultaneous rowdy conversations. Finally he pounded on the coffee table and climbed up on it, putting himself within inches of the ceiling and the painted heart. "Hey, I've got a great idea! We'll all go to Rome for the wedding! I'll get a C-119 and fly everybody down there together! How about that?"

Even the Catholic Chaplain got carried away and shouted, "Dominus Vobiscum!" which meant he was ready for a good stiff libation. The ceremony presumably would be held in the Sistine Chapel, and everyone present was enthusiastic, especially the bride-to-be who beamed showing all her perfect teeth.

Unfortunately, the plans fell through and without the pope's personal blessing; their marriage was doomed to failure. It took an hour for Jim Devorian to remove the spray paint from the ceiling of the BOQ. The marriage took a little longer. The belief is widely held that Angel has been pure ever since.

CHAPTER EIGHT

The Indochina cauldron was bubbling and parties in Kate's quarters continued to grow like a phoenix out of the cigarette ashes of the weekend before—antidotes for hard training and uncertainty. Some of the SFs rotated to CONUS which usually meant Fort Bragg, and others went to assignments in Laos and Thailand, but the aura of the old Park Hotel lingered among the men as shamans passed on their powers to generations after them. They called each other names—passwords to the inner circle, badges earned during various shared exploits which became the stuff of hero tales—Weak Eyes, Pierre, Ice Pick, Giovanni, Jack Frost. Moses, a newly arrived lieutenant, was given his title because he led his SF team out of Austria where they didn't belong, back to "The Promised Land" meaning Bad Tölz and, most particularly, the Enlisted Men's or Officer's Club bar.

As the Sixties began to unfold, developments in Laos, Cambodia, and Vietnam became a deadly game while the French relinquished power in Indochina. During these years Special Forces soldiers worked in a glare of publicity and became known as the Green Berets. On a 1961 visit to the Special Warfare Center in Fort Bragg, a Special Forces group who took a chance and wore unauthorized green berets on parade impressed President Kennedy. Shortly thereafter, Army Regulations authorized the Green Beret as part of the Special Forces uniform. Regular army units already considered the SFs clannish, and the Green Beret, a symbol of eliteness, added insult to injury. Publicity was often more harmful than beneficial as "counterinsurgency" became the new buzzword. Few people understood its meaning.

Old regimes around the world were threatened by Communist takeovers and the mission of 10th Special Forces expanded rapidly beyond

Europe to include North Africa, the Middle East
and South Asia. A variety of missions were
undertaken in the new areas, establishing rap-
port with people in many countries, networks
that later often proved valuable.

Kate heard about one of these missions after
it was over. A U.S. MAAG aircraft crashed in
January in the Zagros Mountains of Iran, killing
four people. Iranian mountain climbers tried to
retrieve the bodies but were unable to reach
them in severe winter conditions. Members of
the German Mountain Division went to Iran, but
also failed. Finally a 10th Special Forces team
headed by two officers succeeded in bringing
down the bodies and even some of their radio
equipment.

One of the officers was the legendary Larry
Thorne (Lauri Torni in Finnish). When
Lieutenant Thorne, a tall, pale-blue-eyed Finn
with muscles of steel, arrived in Bad Tölz, he
was 42 years old and could run circles around
the toughest 21-year-old in the outfit. People
thought twice before opening the door of his
BOQ room in Flint Kaserne. Mountain boots,
guns, ammo, bow and arrows, scuba equipment,
crampons, mountain-climbing ropes, and downhill and cross-country skis were piled wherever
there was space. A dartboard was nailed next to
the door.

He had come to the Green Berets after
extraordinary heroism in the armies of two other
countries. In a fight, ordinary men got out of his
way—rapidly, but he was painfully shy around
women unless he was drinking. For this reason
he was accompanied to parties in the Officer's
Club by a convoy of his fellow officers.

Regulars at weekend gatherings in Kate's
apartment went away on new assignments, some
ferried into Laos by Air America. The White
Star mobile training teams' mission was to train
regular units of the Laotian Army in guerilla
warfare. Kate knew nothing about Laos except

that some of her friends were there, but news of difficulties with too many bosses-the CIA, Laotian government, U.S. State Department, and French advisors—filtered back to military personnel in Flint Kaserne. Sometimes Kate heard rumors in snatches of conversations but made little sense of real events except what was printed in "The Stars & Stripes" or aired on Radio Free Europe broadcasts.

The SFs who lived in primitive conditions among Meo tribesmen in the highlands, far from politics, were able to train an army of 30,000 that was effective until Communists overran it in the '70s. Other SFs trained Kha tribes in the Bolvens Plateau eastward toward Vietnam, an area that contained the southern part of the Ho Chi Minh Trail. The SFs' efforts were negated when Geneva negotiations in 1962 forced withdrawal of all foreign troops from Laos. The North Vietnamese didn't leave.

Kate and other teachers in the American School became aware of new wide-ranging SF interests when their pupils began to bring exotic items for Show and Tell. The children proudly introduced their objects, "Look what my dad brought me!" holding them up high so the back row could see. "He got home last night and was my mother ever glad—and me too!" Unless the owner was too reluctant to let his prize go, the kite from Thailand, Greek doll, beads from Egypt, or bell from Turkey was then passed around among admiring classmates.

When Kate mentioned in the middle of one of her conversations with Ivan, "I wouldn't mind some emerald earrings from Thailand," he snorted and changed the subject.

Pressed for a direct answer, he asked, "Do you think we're going off on damn shopping trips?"

"Of course not." She looked pained. Really, he needed a haircut. "But you could take five minutes off from playing with the natives."

"Don't worry your pretty red head," Ivan retorted. He rearranged the magazines on her coffee table and got up to leave. It was progress of a sort, she decided. Anyway, he was leaving for Berlin, then Fort Bragg in a few days. No need to upset him, so she didn't ask if he was going to Berlin to stop the Soviets from building the wall. Could coming and going end their friendship? Always coming and going. Kate sighed.

The Cuban Missile Crisis, another Communist threat, took headlines in 1962 and the tides of history swirled on without pity into 1963, the year of Kennedy's assassination. Kate would always remember the day. She was late leaving school. It was almost six o'clock. The science teacher and his ninth grade class were in the entrance courtyard pruning bushes, trimming between paving stones, and raking dead leaves from around plantings. The air was strangely silent, not moving. As she drove home, the western sky blazed with lingering red. She rolled her car window down. It was too warm for November in Upper Bavaria. In her apartment she turned the radio on and heard the news from Dallas, Texas.

The calendar changed to 1964 and President Johnson sent troops into Vietnam. The war had started with low profile involvement and advisory missions. It would leave thousands of Americans as mangled flotsam in the rice paddies and jungles of Indochina.

The men didn't talk about the war, but Kate felt an in drawing of breath around her, in the air, intangible. They were suspended, waiting, watching for signs. But everyday life went on—mail came regularly, the commissary was well stocked, movies were scheduled in the theater, and the American Express office was open for business.

There was one noticeable difference. The 10th grew to four times its former size, new fam-

ilies brought so many children, and the
American School expanded into Quonsets and
Army housing attics. More teachers arrived, and
Kate's third grade found the new playground
and gym schedules gave them less time to play.
They saw the music teacher once instead of
twice a week.

A casualty of Vietnam who never went to
that country was Major Robert Boese. In late
1964 Bob was scheduled to leave for Vietnam
and somebody heard him say he didn't expect to
come back. For a lark, his friends gave him an
unusual farewell dinner at the Club. Kate
opened her place card to find his photo looking
grim in a black frame like a funeral notice.
Under the picture were the words "In
Memoriam". This was a little too much black
humor, but Bob laughed rather convincingly,
and everybody except Kate seemed to think the
joke was hilariously funny.

A week before he was scheduled to leave
Bad Tölz, Kate attended a real memorial service
for Major Robert Boese. His helicopter had
crashed on Blomberg Mountain with no survivors.

After the service Kate stopped at the mailroom. There was a letter from Ivan. She tore the
envelope open. The letter was very short, and at
first she didn't believe what it said.

> "Dear Redhead,
>   I know you haven't heard
> from me for a long time. In Nam
> I didn't write anybody, including
> Jim and Hunk, so don't feel left
> out! Back here in the good old
> USA, nobody gives a damn. I
> keep thinking about the Saturday
> sessions in your quarters with all
> the old gang. We understood
> each other.
>   But enough of that. The

world keeps revolving. What I
want to tell you, I've always
wanted to marry you but never
got up the nerve to ask—even
though that must seem out of
character. How about it? You are
and always will be, the only one.
Love, Ivan"

Kate went home and sat down to reread the
letter. She had heard rumors about a French
stripper named Mira in Morristown, New Jersey.
The story was Ivan felt sorry for Mira because
she was down on her luck and he might marry
her. Now this strange letter in her hand.

For a few hours Kate let herself believe marriage to Ivan would work. Then her survival
instincts triumphed, and she wrote him a sensi-
ble letter explaining in essence that they'd probably kill each other after no more than a day of
wedlock. That was that, but the question stayed
in her mind.

In October 1965, disbelief followed the
news in 10th Special Forces that Major Larry A.
Thorne was missing on the Ho Chi Minh Trail
and presumed dead. He was the invincible war-
rior and some day he would come striding out of
the jungle swearing mightily in Finnish or
German or Russian or fractured English. Unlike
the soldiers with him, his body was never
found—Gulliver lost forever in the land of the
Lilliputans.

CHAPTER NINE

Ivan pushed his elbows into the bar like jello trying to find a center of gravity. He was on the last drink before his flight left from an American air base outside London when she came in, a gorgeous brunette with eyelashes long enough to hang your green beret on. But then he saw the guy following her and it was a goddam general, three star and old enough to be her father. He ordered two more on the rocks and then two more, and finally somebody poured him into a car from the motor pool, which took him to the airstrip hangar. An MP at the departure gate looked at his orders and saw that he was headed for a B-29 flight already in the air. He put down the phone. "It's gone, Colonel," he said, pointing up. "You'll be staying in the VIP quarters tonight, sir. We'll put you on tomorrow's manifest."

Ivan managed the Hollywood version of a salute, allowed himself to be taken to his quarters and mustered enough strength when he got there to select a small bottle of scotch among those in the refrigerator.

So, Lieutenant Colonel "Ivan" Robert Herrick had a good night's sleep, not knowing the plane he was supposed to take had crashed in the mountains near Stuttgart with no survivors.

The news the next day put him on a plane in fairly sober condition. But by the time he arrived in Stuttgart and on to Neubiberg with everyone treating him like a ghost returned from the dead, he was definitely in the mood for a drink. He picked up his VW at the airfield on the edge of Munich and drove south along the Autobahn, turning off at Holzkirchen. There he took the country road to the Special Forces Base outside Bad Tölz. Instead of stopping at Kate's, he decided to go first to the Officer's Club and see how his buddies reacted to his miraculous escape. This took quite awhile because everybody agreed they should celebrate the fact he had had too much to drink the night before.

It was after closing hours when the bartender finally had enough. "Come on, guys, I'm lockin' up this place and goin' home!" But Ivan wasn't quite ready to call it a day.

At midnight, when Kate opened her door, she found him leaning on the doorbell leering at her. His eyes weren't tracking straight. "Can I come in?"

She stared at him icily for a long moment and finally stated without any particular venom. "You're drunk. Go away."

With great effort he pulled himself up as nearly to his full six feet two as he could and saluted, "I'm a ver-r-r-y lucky person. Wanna hear more?" She shut the door in his face and heard him swearing and stumbling down the sidewalk. Just as she was turning out the light, a car engine started with a roar. Then she heard a crash and silence.

"Damn!" Kate groaned. "He's hit my car!" Sure enough, the VW was making mad love with her Chevy, and it looked like a permanent liaison. A giggle in her throat burst, and she went out of control laughing. Wouldn't do any good to cry. Ivan was weaving a zigzag course up the hill toward the Bachelor Officers Quarters.

Even though there was nothing she could do about the car until morning, Kate could not go to sleep and her mind went back to the early Fifties. LIFE in capital letters had begun with the Park Hotel, home to single officers, transients, single teachers in the American Army Dependents School, and a few secretaries. Although the hotel was in the middle of Bad Tölz, it was also the Officer's Club for Flint Kaserne, the American Base on the eastern limits of the town. Kate, with other singles, had long since been moved to the Kaserne. But all those lucky enough to be billeted in the hotel

during the few years of its existence would
never forget its ramshackle appearance, the
smell of dust, wet mops and old cooking grease,
bathrooms down the hall, and quartermaster furniture with ten coats of black varnish. Famous
all over the European Command for its lively
occupants, the hotel's creaky stairs kept
nobody's secrets. The American officer in
charge had to have a good sense of humor. He
was also airborne which helped.

Kate grinned in the dark remembering the
Friday night in 1955 when she first met Ivan. He
had thought because she was a schoolteacher she
could be easily shocked. Her third graders knew
better, but it took Ivan a couple of tries before he
figured it out.

Kate thought about the Green Berets. They
were a different breed, a lot more complex than
their rambunctious exteriors revealed. Life to
them seemed very short and every moment
counted double. That was part of it. The rest
wasn't so easy— something about the way their
jump boots walked and how they wore the
Green Beret, careless but at the right angle so
you knew it mattered.

The originals were already legends when
they arrived in Bad Tölz with the 10th Special
Forces Group, Airborne. Handpicked by
Colonel Aaron Bank, founder of the unit and
their first Commanding Officer, the originals
were from Airborne units seasoned in Sicily,
Monte Cassino, Ste.-Mère-Eglise, the Battle of
the Bulge and the bitter winds of Korea.

Colonel Bank was one of the legends, O.S.S.
with the French Resistance. He was a leader in
"Operation Iron Cross", the plot to assassinate
Hitler, and he knew Ho Chi Minh in Indochina.

And others like Captain John Scagnelli—
now there was a real original—a rough tough
paratrooper with a crackle voice like Clark
Gable, who saw it all from Salerno through
Britain and across Germany, to some of the

worst fighting in Korea. Old timers who had known him in action would rather go into battle with THE SCAG than any soldier they'd ever met. Love wasn't too big a word for what they thought of him—a soldier's soldier. Kate smiled to herself.

Punching her pillow into shape, she remembered the evening when the advance party of the 10th Special Forces Group, Airborne, sauntered into the Park Hotel bar, taking their time, sizing it up. She saw the scene as Edward Hopper would paint it—a corner of the room where four teachers are playing bridge in a dusty amber pool of light from a floor lamp, the rest of the big room in shadows except for Millie behind the bar, and the SFs caught in mid-stride just inside the doorway, curious, investigating this alien group of card players. No money on the table?! Right. From a different world. They move on to the bar. The first big scene of Camelot, where fact and fiction blend into each other and become the same story—a remarkable time understood only in retrospect.

At 0300 hrs. Kate turned off the light for the third time and peered out the window, imagining a gray pre-dawn light spilling over the eastern rim of the valley. It was very quiet. Then she heard the rumble of a truck driving out of the Kaserne gate with a load of men and equipment.

CHAPTER TEN

Ivan boarded the charter jet in Travis Air Force Base with the old feeling of anxiety. He had long since given up trying to persuade himself that flying without a parachute was safe. He knew from experience how far down it was, and short and messy without a chute. His recent escape because he was on the wrong flight out of an airbase in England had done nothing to allay his suspicion that he might be running out of miracles.

This time, in 1967, the fourteen-hour flight over the Arctic Circle was uneventful, just long and boring. His mind had plenty of time between mediocre meals and trips to the john to remember his last tour in Nam. He'd lost a good buddy in the Io Drang operation.

"Counterinsurgency" was still the buzz word echoing around the Pentagon when he had looked up a few friends on his way through D.C. Trouble was, nobody in the higher echelons of Washington seemed to have the slightest idea what the word meant in terms of dead men. Just a word to bruit about when there was a lull in the conversation. Ivan's thoughts were bitter. Hell, the old timer SFs knew better. He closed his eyes. Until he hit Saigon, he was only arguing with himself. Save the heavy stuff 'til he got there.

It was late September and in Bad Tölz the sun would be setting earlier behind the mountains. There might even be a thin veil of snow on the Brauneck, prelude to the winter ski season. Kate was back in school with the ankle biters. What day was it there? He did a fast calculation and decided she was probably somewhere in Friday while he was already starting Saturday. He looked down and saw the morning sun catching serpent curves of brown water in the Mekong Delta. At least it wasn't raining. The jet was approaching Saigon from the west, and he had a glimpse of Rung Sat. He had once waded through that swamp for what seemed endless days of misery. Must have been his second tour.

A few minutes later they circled in for a landing at the Tan Son Nhut Air Base in Saigon. The wheels bumped twice. The pilot gunned the engine; let it take control, braked slowly and the plane rolled to a stop. Ivan stood up, stretching wearily. His shoulders ached and his legs felt like heavy wooden stilts. Inactivity was hell. Maybe he'd find a massage parlor in Cholon—a quick way to tone up sore muscles. He thought it might have other advantages as well, but with some risks attached.

At check-in he was told his orders were changed to Nha Trang, 5th Special Forces Headquarters, Logistics, and there was just time to catch lunch at the Club before the next C-130 took off for Danang with a stop at Nha Trang on the way. Ivan shook his head. "No, Sarge. Please, just send them a message I'm coming up tomorrow. You do have aircraft going tomorrow?"

"Yes sir, Colonel Herrick." The sergeant looked at Ivan and sighed. "Consider it done. I'll put you on the one leaving at 1000 hrs."

Ivan glanced at the sergeant's nametag. "Thanks, Sergeant Ruskin. I appreciate it." Who the hell had changed his orders? At least he'd be far away from Saigon politics. Ivan picked up his baggage and took a cab to the BOQ where his rank got him a very decent room. At the moment, all that interested him was a hot shower and a reasonably comfortable bed. He sat down on the edge of the bed and took his boots off. His feet were rarely warm. Poor circulation from wearing the damn boots. He supposed they had saved him from far worse trouble.

It was late afternoon when Ivan awoke. For a second he wondered where he was. Then he remembered. Time for a drink or two before dinner.

He cleaned up, shaved, and decided to walk
to the Club. It felt good to stretch his legs.
There'd been some changes since his last tour in
Nam. The Club was newly decorated with a
thick beige carpet, more mirrors behind the bar
and some oil paintings of the New York skyline
and the Grand Canyon. "I wonder what the tax-
payers paid for those," he was thinking when
someone put a hand on his shoulder. He turned
to find Sam, an Air Force major he had known
as a lieutenant in the Air Force Survival School
in Flint Kaserne. "How long has it been?" The
two shook hands.
        "'54 in Tölz."
        "Right."
        "What are you doing here, Sam?"
        "Leaving for Travis tomorrow morning. It's
about time!"
        "Ships that pass in the night. I just came
from there. Tomorrow it's on to 5th
Headquarters, Logistics at Nha Trang and who
knows where else. They're keeping it for a surprise." The two men laughed.
        They finished their drinks and went into the
dining room for the usual steak, French fries,
caesar salad, and over-cooked green beans,
which they both left on their plates. A combo
was playing oldies in the background, and Ivan
and Sam looked at each other with the same
idea. "Let's get out of here," offered Sam. "It's
my last night in this exciting Paris of the East.
Might as well take a last look at the bright
lights."
        Off Base, garish electric signs blinked on
and off, coloring crowded streets and traffic with
splashes of crimson, yellow, green and purple.
Hawkers shouted the high quality of their t-
shirts in Pidgin English. Panels of black velvet
painted with gold elephants, U.S. Army insignia
or "I LOv u Mothr", as well as more earthy messages hung on racks and swung from lines on the
outer walls of shanties. Beggars, heavily made-

up young prostitutes in scant clothing swinging
their fringed skirts, and a maelstrom of old cars,
bicycles and three-wheeled pedicabs jammed
narrow streets and alleys.

Near the Base guard post the two Americans
had found a rickety French taxi made of a variety of unrelated parts. The Vietnamese driver
threaded his dilapidated car through the tangle,
shouting and honking the horn continuously. On
the side of the road a young American GI was
propped up against a half-opened door, which
revealed part of a haze-filled room with cubicles
and dim figures. "He's been smoking white poi-
son. Forgot the buddy system." Sam shook his
head. "North Vietnam is pouring pure cocaine
into GI night spots every day. It's going to win
the war."

"It's one of the big problems," agreed Ivan.

They stopped their taxi to pick up the GI and
deliver him back to the Base, but Military Police
in a jeep pulled up behind them, scooped him
up, and went into the building behind him, looking for more Americans.

"The kid will probably be back tomorrow if
he's not locked up," remarked Ivan, yawning.

"You've got that right," said Sam. "Not
much to see out here except traffic jams. We
might as well go back to the Base and get some
shut-eye before dawn breaks like thunder over
the bay."

By a miracle their driver returned them to
the Base without accident, and Sam held out his
hand. "Leaving early so I'll probably miss you
at breakfast. Great seeing you, Ivan. Good luck."

"Same to you. Good trip home," answered
Ivan and headed for the Officer's Club bar.

The next morning Ivan's flight was delayed
but landed in Nha Trang shortly after noon. The
NCO who met him confirmed that he was
expected in SF Headquarters. The NCO would
drive him there and then take care of his baggage as soon as he met another C-130 coming in

with bales of barbed wire and other supplies
needed by the A camps. "How's the supply system working?" asked Ivan.

"Pretty good, sir." The NCO whose name
was Daniels, shrugged. "That's not the problem.
We're low on manpower, especially manpower
to work with MIKE groups. Our Headquarters in
Saigon is right. They keep sending boys over
here still wet behind the ears. What's the matter
with the Pentagon?" he exploded. "Don't they
know we need men, real men? Chri-i-st!"

"I think they're beginning to wise up,
Daniels." Ivan tried to sound optimistic. "As you
know, it's slow work to train volunteers for
Special Forces. A lot of the ones who volunteer
can't hack it, which surprises the hell out of the
generals. Most of them don't know what we do,
or don't want to know. What we need are more
NCOs like you with experience in the field, not
secondhand from textbooks." Ivan stopped.
Why jaw on about something they both knew.

On the way to Headquarters, he asked questions—how many camps were ready in case of
attack? Defense perimeters secure? CIDG personnel adequate? Communications tested?
Morale in the camps? Ammunition stockpiled?
Helicopter back up? —And other concerns
which would prepare him for briefings. Daniels'
replies were succinct and showed a practical
grasp of priority problems beyond his supply
MOS. Ivan was proud that men like Daniels
filled the ranks of Special Forces. Each one
knew his safety depended on the reliability and
training of every other member of the team. He
was in the center of a network of close brothers—an elite group. At the first opportunity, he
would ask what date Jim Devorian was expected to arrive in Nam and where he was assigned.
He'd heard Jim was coming in any day now.
Maybe they could both get R & R in Saigon or
Hué.

They arrived at HQ and Daniels drove past a

row of barracks and large white warehouses to
the commander's office. Ivan was waved in after
a short wait. The first thing he saw was a poster-
size photograph of the colonel dropping through
clouds under his parachute. The photo dominat-
ed the wall behind the desk where Colonel
Wright was now sitting—not the hallmark of an
original Green Beret. No original had to impress
anybody.

Ivan had known Colonel Wright for only a
short time at the Psych Warfare School in Bragg.
He remembered the man as a smart, feisty officer with strong opinions and no hesitation about
voicing them, the kind of guy who worked on
Sunday and expected everybody else to do the
same. His date-of-rank was only eleven months
earlier than Ivan's.

His handshake was firm. "Glad to have you
here, Colonel Herrick. Long time no see. You've
been in this hellhole before so I don't need to tell
you much except what's been going on recently.
You know the Pentagon-Washington part of the
story. I disagree with some of the details. If the
big shots who come here and use up chopper
time would get down and dirty, they'd have
more idea what's going on, but I suppose you
already know that."

"Yes," Ivan answered. "I have seen some
evidence of it. They're never interested in bad
news."

"You're Goddamed right!" Colonel Wright
went on. "We need a lot more well-trained SFs
than they're sending over here. Most of them
can jump out of aircraft and some know French
or a smattering of Vietnamese, enough to get in
trouble, but all of them miss experience, and
that's what counts in this war. What I wouldn't
give for a bunch of the originals. Thank God
you're one of them!" And he proceeded to brief
Ivan on current plans and weak areas that needed attention.

Colonel Wright ended with the real zinger.

Ivan was to go to forward camps, especially in isolated positions near the Cambodian border, and assess what needed to be done. He was to set priorities and make plans to fix what needed to be fixed. The job was to be accomplished in the shortest time possible, like yesterday. Ivan snapped to attention. "Yes SIR!"

Colonel Wright grinned broadly, reaching across his desk to give Ivan a sheaf of papers. He accompanied Ivan to the door, shook his hand once more and pointed. "Major Dunlop will give you a briefing. Down the hall to your right."

As he left the office, Ivan looked for Captain Queeg's palm tree. Nothing growing in sight.

CHAPTER ELEVEN

The Green Berets' best advocate, John F.Kennedy, had been gone for almost four years and conventional warfare officers in the Pentagon were not amused by Special Forces' unorthodox ways. As Jim Devorian put it, "They won't let us win this shit war and they won't let us lose it!"

"Who's they?" asked Kate.

"A lot of great white hunters sitting behind desks, writing memorandums and screwing their secretaries," answered Devorian—adding, after some reflection, "Well, maybe not. Might be their junior officers' wives. Yeah! You know what? We ain't got no spit and polish—as if that matters in hell when you're surrounded by VC, and your ammo's running low!"

"If it's so lousy, why don't you get out or find yourself a club officer job in Saigon?"

Devorian regarded her a long moment without seeing her. "I guess some have, but most of us wouldn't desert our buddies just because the chopper's going down—." He grinned, "Unless we've got a chute!" For a second he was his old self.

Kate held her breath and let it out slowly, wishing she hadn't asked. It was one of the few times they talked about Vietnam. She poured him a drink and tried to hold the moment. "The gang will probably be over here tomorrow night. Are you coming?"

They were in Kate's apartment, one of the Friday nights no one else was there. She wasn't sure he was listening, rubbing his hand over his forehead, a habit he had when he was disturbed about something. She waited but he didn't answer. A little silence lengthened into minutes and then from the sofa where his long frame was sprawled, he reached for his glass on the floor. "Kate, I'm on leave this weekend and it's the last one before I head for Nam again. I need to get away from the rat race for just a couple of days. Could you possibly pull up stakes and go down to Garmisch with me?" adding hastily, "I'm not talking anything significant here."

"The wolf visiting grandma couldn't have put it better." They both laughed and the momentary tension was broken.

"You should get away too," he said, "somewhere the ankle biters won't be hollering `Hello-o Miss O'Brien! Ma, there's Miss O'Brien!'"

"You're so right. When'll we go and when will we come back? Have to come back, you know, take up our burdens!"

Devorian pulled himself upright. "Good girl! I'll pick you up around 1000 in the morning—call for a couple of rooms at the Eibsee—back Sunday night. Bring a glad rag. We're going to a top-of-the-line restaurant." Jim was a dear, dear friend, and Kate felt extraordinarily pleased with life in general.

Saturday was dark and foggy, but as they took a detour to Oberammergau, the clouds began to thin. They passed a hayfield and a double rainbow formed, drenching the field with colors. Jim stopped the car and pulled a camera out of his bag. "I want your picture with that background." She smiled into the camera from the roadside, her red hair catching glints of opal mist. "It's a good omen," he beamed and lingered a moment before putting the camera away.

The rain started again but by the time they were in Oberammergau eating lunch, the sun broke through and turned the high meadows and trees to electric green. "There's no tomorrow, Jim," she said, squeezing his arm.

"No tomorrow," he echoed, stopping to look past the painted houses to the uplands and rock formations around the village. "This is good for sore eyes. No worries and my best girl friend with me. I'll race you to the car!"

"You win. I'm not running after eating that plateful of Bauernomelet."

The road spiraling down from Ettal Monastery took them into the outskirts of Garmisch Partenkirchen and the usual traffic snarl. The Zugspitze, part of a mountain range on the edge of Austria and the highest mountain in Germany, towered above a cluster of shops and Alpine-style houses. The town was an American Rest and Recreation Center and they went to the Billeting Office to get their reservations for the Eibsee Hotel, an Army hotel in the mountains above Garmisch.

"Wanna play a short game of golf before we settle in up there?"

"Why not," she agreed. As they drove through town and parked by the Rec Center Golf Course, Kate studied his serious face with laugh lines around the eyes, some premature gray in his hair, the lean, hard-muscled body—a gentle giant.

Devorian felt her concentration and, when they reached the starting point, he asked, "Hey, darlin'! Are we having fun or what?"

She set the ball for her first drive. "I'll let you know when I get a hole in one!" Her dark red hair was shining in the mid-afternoon sun. He'd never seen it like that before. Oh hell!

Their rooms at the Eibsee faced the lake and they were in time to see the sun sink, spilling red into the water. Looking at it, a chill tingled down her spine. The room seemed cold. She said, "Should I go dressy for dinner? Where are we going?"

Jim was lingering in the doorway. "Let's have a glass of wine before we head back into Garmisch. We'll go to the Post for dinner."

"The Post? Isn't that a German hotel now?"

"Yeah. It's renovated and really top class."

"Isn't it pretty expensive?"

"Don't worry leetle one. Your old uncle has plenty big money! You can't believe!"

Kate hadn't seen him like this for a long time. It promised to be a special evening with one of her favorite men.

In the Eibsee lounge, Devorian studied her over their wine glasses. They'd never been alone together before, away from Tölz or a crowd of Green Berets, and he felt a surge of feeling. She's Ivan's girl, he warned himself. Keep it light. The candle on their table made her eyes seem greener than gray, and her long hair called for touching. Kate was tall, almost as tall as he was, but tonight she looked small and vulnerable in a green dress that was clingy in all the right places. Damn it to hell!

She was looking at his hands. They were big hands that should be clumsy but weren't. They were steady, dependable hands that could hold a delicate wine glass and also—

"This wine is powerful stuff!" they said almost in unison. Jim put her coat around her, and they drove slowly down the winding road to Garmisch where they dined on gourmet "Steak Americain" with all the artful trimmings by the best chef in town.

"I'm purring." She smiled at him over Pear Helene.

"You look like the cat's meow, leetle Mitzi! Now let's see if Max Gregor's band is still in town."

Dancing had never been like this. They seemed to be doing unfamiliar steps and moving as if they'd practiced for years, instinctively knowing what came next. "Tell me, Jim, is it the wine or are we actually floating about three inches off the floor?"

"No girl. You're really riding around on my feet." She looked down and he laughed, pulling her closer.

At 0100 hours the band played "Aufwiedersehen" and they left reluctantly, walking out to the car holding hands. His blood was drumming danger, and he took a gulp of cold air to quiet himself. He had no clue what she was thinking.

He drove up to the Eibsee almost in silence, his hand still touching hers. At her room they stopped while he unlocked the door and stood leaning against it, one arm around her. His eyes darkened. He looked down at her. "Do you belong to Ivan?" he asked.

"No." It sounded like a promise.

"Do you want me to stay?"

"Yes," she said simply. Threads of light came through the shutters from the lamps along the lakeshore, deepening the shadows in the room. "This is crazy," she whispered. They did not turn on the light.

Doris C. Baker

CHAPTER TWELVE

In the morning Devorian awoke to the splash of the shower and called, "Kate! Come here, leetle one!" She appeared in an old flannel robe with her hair still damp, looking like a teenager. "Come closer, the better to see you, my dear!"

"You've been reading Little Red Riding Hood again." She sat on the edge of the bed smiling, and then traced his cheekbone with her finger.

Jim was serious, pulling her closer. "So little time. Why did it take so damn long? If we could go back to the first time we met and develop a long together-history—have to make up now for lost time." Her skin was warm, soap-scented—soft. He stopped talking.

Ravenous and craving black coffee, they made it to the dining room just before it closed. "Check-out time is noon, but I'm going to ask the desk clerk to let us keep our rooms until tomorrow. We can get up early and drive back to Tölz before you have to go to school. I'm so short, only a few days left, they could care less if I check in on time or not. OK?"

"You know it's OK."

"Yes I do." He touched her hand. "C'mon. Let's take a walk along the lake. It's windy so we'd better wear all the clothes we brought along. But I don't think the green dress you wore last night would do you much good."

The sun was sparkling on the Eibsee, wind-driven waves whipping across the lake. The effect was dazzling. Devorian went back to get their sunglasses and they walked briskly arms linked. "In spite of being friends so long, we don't know much about each other Before Bad Tölz—B.B.T. What were you like when you were a little girl?" It was his voice, not the cold that was sending shivers inside her.

"I was a tomboy or my mother thought so. I grew up on a ranch in Wyoming and rode horses with the ranch hands when I was still a kid. My father didn't have much time for me, and then he died in an accident when I was eighteen. My mother tried to keep the ranch going but had to give up and sell it. Good I finished college and got a job teaching before our money ran out." Kate stopped for a minute and then went on. "She's gone now too, so I've been on my own for awhile. What about you?"

"Not much to tell." He bent over and skipped a pebble across the bright water. "My folks were immigrants from Lebanon. They had cousins in New York who told them to come to the land of milk and honey, but it was a long time before they had any honey. Their cousins gave them a roof over their heads and the basic necessities until they got started in the restaurant business. First it was a greasy spoon, then a franchise chain, and finally a real restaurant with Lebanese specialties. They'd 've made a lot more money if all the relatives hadn't eaten there for free."

"Where are they now?" asked Kate.

"Somebody made 'em an offer they couldn't refuse, and they're retired on Long Island enjoying their grandchildren." Seeing Kate's expression, he added, "Oh, they're not mine. My brother has three." Her eyes still had a question, and he answered it. "I was married once. She was a nice Lebanese girl and my folks still haven't forgiven us for divorcing, but we had nothing in common. In fact, she found someone else before we were divorced. It didn't make any difference. I didn't care."

They were out of sight of the hotel. He turned suddenly and put his arms around her, holding her so close they created a single shadow. "Could you wait for me, Kate? I want to marry you and forever is what I mean." They stood still together in the icy wind. She would never forget the moment—the warm protection of his arms around her, sun flashing on the water, and the ring of White Mountains circling them in the middle of the world. Forever seemed possible.

"Yes, Jim. Forever and forever."

Their faces were stinging from the cold, and they turned their backs to the west wind, retracing their steps to the hotel, walking faster. "Have we a plan for today?" asked Kate. "Not that it matters."

"How about Sunday dinner at the Post in Wallgau? We can eat on the balcony. It used to be a hayloft in the barn and the food is great—solid but great."

"I'd love it. Can't believe I'm hungry. It's all this fresh air—and—" They looked at each other and laughed.

"We'll celebrate. I feel like celebrating. We'll have a good bottle of champagne—pretend it's our wedding day."

He brushed a kiss on her cheek and she thought, bad luck. We're going too fast, but covered her fear saying, "I love you—love you, Jim, —"

"Tell me again. I want to hear it again."

The dinner was as good as expected; a very expensive bottle of champagne washed away her misgivings, and the ice show at the Casa Carioca ended the day that was gone too quickly. After a few dances they were sitting at their table, an intent look in her eyes watching the dancers. Jim winced, wondering if her thoughts were about Ivan.

As if she'd read his mind, she put her hand on his. "I'm memorizing this minute, every second of it." Devorian signaled for the check—time to go. He drove back to the hotel faster around the curves than was really wise.

"Are you happy?" he asked a little later, anxious to hear her say it. She was silent and he thought she was asleep, but she said, "Why don't we just go to Spain or some oasis in the Sahara Desert and forget what we're supposed to do?"

"God!" He groaned and paused, trying to sound cheerful. "Well—we've got four more days—and nights—count 'em one by one, minute by minute. Can you believe it? We just missed not having this at all!" His voice was uneven.

When Kate came home from school Monday, he was waiting for her. The day had been hectic as days often were when the Föhn wind blew. It had been hard to keep the roof on her classroom.

"I've got something for you, Little Red," he said, throwing his jacket and beret on a chair. "Not going to gobble you up—not just yet anyway—although I'd like to—."

She was getting that funny feeling inside. Wrong, wrong, she thought. Think of ice—or—shoveling snow. He opened the little box in his hand. "This is Eichmann's best. Some day we'll go to Tiffany's, but right now we have to do things faster than most people," and he took a diamond solitaire out of the box. She caught her breath. "Kathryn O'Brien, I want this to remind you every day that I love you. Will you marry me?"

It was a proper proposal, as if they had been in love for a long time, and she answered in kind. "Yes, Jim, I'll wear it all my life and love you all my life." She felt as if she had a raging fever. The ring was fire burning her hand.

He said slowly, "Let's go see the chaplain tomorrow early and find out if there's any way to get around German law. We can't wait weeks for a marriage license. Could you be ready for a wedding on Friday?"

"A shotgun wedding! How about today?" She hugged him, laughing, and he swung her across the room in a swooping tango, coming to a halt just before they crashed into the bookcase. His words were sobering.

"Don't count on it. The Germans are sticklers for rules, you know."

Tuesday morning, when the Protestant chaplain arrived at his office, they were waiting for him. It was a bare little room below the chapel with two small desks and a few folding chairs serving both Protestant and Catholic chaplains. The chaplain's first question caught them by surprise. "Do you believe in God?" To fill the silence Kate answered, "You're his representative and you're our hope to be married before Jim leaves for Vietnam Saturday."

The chaplain waited. It was Devorian's turn. "There must be something—a plan—. Life is too complicated to be just a blind accident—just for nothing. You're a paratrooper, Chaplain. You've seen combat. I'm sure you know what I mean."

"I only want to know whether you respect the sacrament of the church, or if this sudden rush to marry is from an impulsive wish." The chaplain looked at the two anxious faces a long moment and then added, "Don't get your hopes up, but in the circumstances I'll see what I can do. There's a local official downtown, a friend of mine, who may be able to help. I'll let you know later today."

As it turned out, the local official was sympathetic and had the right connections in Kreis Stadt Wolfratshausen where permissions for marriage licenses were issued. That night their friends began preparations for the wedding on Friday, Devorian's last day in Bad Tölz.

They did their best, Kate and Jim, to delay time, walking forest paths to the lake behind Reutberg Monastery, exploring trails and valleys new to her above Lenggries, trying mostly unsuccessful jokes. By Wednesday afternoon Jim saw that Kate was exhausted, and they stopped in Waldherralm, a small Hütte near a mountain trail. He ordered Wienerbrot and two Grünerbrau beers, but Kate asked for coffee instead, afraid a beer would send her into a crying jag. That wouldn't do at all.

Jim looked over the top of his glass at her. "Kate, I've written my family all about you so they'll soon know how lucky I am. Here's the photo I sent them of you under the double rainbow. This one's for you, and I have one to keep with me. They'll see how beautiful you are. Write to them—but write to me first! I know they'll telephone more often than they write. At their age it's easier."

She put out her hand to him. "Of course I'll write to them. I hope they'll like me." He covered her hand with his, and they discovered a blob of mustard greasing both their palms. Laughter and wiping up the mess with paper napkins took them past another silence.

Nothing slowed the hours until the last day was upon them—a flurry of two wedding ceremonies, one civil and one religious. There had been no time for shopping trips so Kate borrowed a new silk dress Helen's sister had just sent her from the States. It was pale beige, almost ivory, and every one agreed they had never seen such a beautiful bride.

While their guests left the chapel to gather at Dave and Helen's quarters for the reception, Kate and Jim called his parents in Long Island. Their talk was awkward at first until Jim's mother started to cry. "Oh Jimmy, we wish we could be there to hug and kiss you both!"

"I know, ma, there just wasn't enough time."

His father came on the phone. "We're drinking some really good champagne over here, son. When are we going to see the two of you and celebrate big time with the whole family?"

"Soon, pop, soon! You're going to love Kate. Keep the letters coming. I'll write you the address. We just wish you were here with us instead of so far away. Hugs and kisses to you and the rest of the family."

Jim put down the phone and turned to Kate. "Come on, dearest girl, to the first party of our married life."

  As they walked in the door, a chorus of good wishes greeted them, Dave's voice heard above the rest. "Did you get lost? We were about to send out a search and rescue team." He handed them each a glass of champagne, and the guests drank the first toast to Kate and Jim's future happiness together.

  Their friends tried hard to make the reception a happy occasion with plenty of champagne punch, and almost succeeded. Finally, at midnight, everybody had gone home. Dave was helping Helen wash dishes and clean up the kitchen. She gave the counter a swipe with the dishcloth and looked at her husband for a long moment. "Dave, love, did you feel like we were entertaining at a wake?"

  "Don't say it out loud for God's sake!"

  Helen put her arms around him and they held each other tight.

  Jim had to catch a flight out of Neubiberg to Frankfurt at 0700 hours so it was still dark as Kate lay in bed listening to sounds of him in the shower, shaving, and putting the last gear in his baggage. This was even worse than she had expected.

  He came back to her. "Okay, girl, it'll seem like forever but really not long 'til I'm holding you close like this again. We'll be an old married couple!" His voice was unsteady.

  "I love you," was all she could manage. The door closed and he was gone. She had only dry tears, clenching her fists until the nails bit into her palms. That afternoon and every Saturday, a dozen red roses were delivered to her door with a card, "I love you. Jim."

CHAPTER THIRTEEN

Kate came home to her quarters Friday after
school tired, not sure she could face another
friendly weekend invasion. Last week an inebri-
ated man from Munich HQ Criminal
Investigation Detachment had staggered into a
gathering in her living room and fallen into the
shelves with her Kufstein glass collection. Every
piece except one wine glass was smashed. After
Hunk deposited him outdoors, the man had wandered back into her hallway and taken a
Venetian glass clown away with him. Kate discovered the loss when the others were leaving.
In less than five minutes, her SF friends
swarmed into his BOQ room, picked up the
clown with some threats pertaining to the man's
future health, and brought the clown back to
Kate.

Major Peter Gulden, a newcomer to the 10th,
viewed these proceedings with quiet amuse-
ment, but found a broom and cleaned up the broken glass before anyone else thought of it. The
P.T.A. president, a captain in the Lenggries
Quartermaster School, arrived in the middle of
the excitement bringing Kate a pile of P.T.A.
notices to take to school. He was greeted by a
loud chorus, "Here's a Goddamn LEG!!" which
didn't seem to upset him, but Kate noticed that
Peter diverted his attention by pouring him a
stiff drink.

He's an observer like me, Kate thought, and
he has unusual social grace in the middle of a
bunch of good-time guys on the loose. With that
physique, nobody'll tangle with him!

Now a week had gone by and here was Peter
at her door asking if she wanted to go into
Munich for dinner—"If you don't think Jim
would mind. I just need some companionship!"

She realized she was looking her worst,
probably covered with chalk dust and feeling
crabby and exhausted after an hour-long confer-

ence with the parent of a problem child. "I'm a mess." She hesitated. "But if you're not in a hurry—"

"No, no. The place I have in mind is for night owls, so you have all the time you want. It's small, but the French chef there is very good and the wine cellar is excellent. I hope you'll enjoy it."

In a hot shower her headache disappeared, and she searched through her wardrobe for something to match the occasion. They were definitely not going to the Hofbrauhaus.

Promptly at 1945 hours Peter came for her in a Jaguar sports car, leaving her speechless for some seconds. "I'm impressed!" she blurted. "Are you a millionaire or did you steal it?"

"Neither one." He looked rather pleased with himself. "My father is an importer in Amsterdam, and he bought it for himself then decided to give it to me when I was assigned to a European base. It's a little ostentatious but I couldn't refuse without hurting his feelings, hm-m-m? It's a dream on the road. Want to drive?"

"Heavens no! Is your family Dutch? How did you get in the Green Berets?"

"So many questions. I'll tell all over dinner; right now let's put it up to speed. I'm hungry."

When they reached the restaurant on Maximilianstrasse the opera crowd was going in, and she realized it had taken half of the usual hour to drive to Munich. Their table was by a window overlooking the street, and crowds of Müncheners were walking by. Peter watched Kate with pleasure. She had so much sparkle, this girl—no pseudo sophisticated chatter. She was wearing Jim's ring, and he reached over and took her hand. "I know you're in love and you look it! Jim Devorian is a great guy, and he's lucky besides."

He ordered a light wine to go with the first course, and they began to talk. Peter's father had owned a spice plantation in Vietnam, and he had grown up with the children of French plantation owners and their workers.

"What was your mother like?" Kate asked.

Peter's blue eyes were faraway. "She never really wanted to live on the plantation, hated the climate, and spent part of the year in the Netherlands. That meant I had to go with her until I was old enough to help my father manage the plantation. Amsterdam and the family home seemed like prison after the freedom in Vietnam. I can still see her propped up on her pillows under the ceiling fan when we were in Vietnam, directing the maids in their household chores. Afternoons I'd come from French school and find her entertaining other European wives at tea. I was glad to escape to my homework."

He stopped. Kate leaned forward sipping her wine and he continued. "I never wanted to take over the plantation. When I was old enough I joined the Foreign Legion. Then a friend in Fort Bragg got me interested in the Green Berets, and here I am."

Peter picked up his glass. "I've been doing all the talking and I'm usually so quiet!" He added softly, "You have a real talent with people—and you look lovely, Kate. There's a good orchestra at the Excelsior. How about it? I'm not ready to go home. Are you?"

"All right." She tried to sound enthusiastic and failed. She wanted very much to go home.

His eyes were probing. "Would you rather call it an evening?" he asked smoothly. "You must be tired after teaching all day. I understand, and you miss your husband."

He didn't understand. No one could. But she didn't want to spoil his evening, so she went along to the Excelsior trying to pretend he was Jim, which was quite useless. After a few dances they started back to Tölz. Traffic was light on the Autobahn and when they turned off, the little villages along the way faded into the dark. The hour hand on the dashboard showed eleven o'clock, but it seemed later to Kate.

At her door Peter said, "Thank you for the evening, Kate. Good night, my dear." He kissed her hand and the Jaguar went up the hill and out of the Kaserne. She wondered what the other Green Berets thought of him. He made you feel like a princess and at the same time a little uncomfortable as if he could tell what you were thinking. She wrote Jim a long letter and went to bed, but she had a hard time falling asleep. The next day was Saturday and a dozen red roses from Jim were delivered to her door, just as they had been every Saturday since he left.

CHAPTER FOURTEEN

Colonel Robert "Ivan" Herrick was having his usual Scotch before dinner at the Officer's Club in Hué, celebrating his few days of R & R, but mostly thinking about the letter from Dave and Helen. It had arrived that afternoon at mail call. He was having difficulty focusing on the letter's opening, "You won't believe this. Kate and Jim are going to be married tomorrow!"

The letter went on with details, but he concentrated on the first two sentences, making a major effort. They were right. He couldn't believe it. In fact, it didn't make the slightest sense. Devorian and Kate had been pals like they were all buddies 'til hell froze over. But married. Not possible. It was probably a half-assed joke. He'd read the rest of it later for a good laugh. Ivan stuffed the letter into his pocket and ordered another Scotch, but before the drink was in front of him, pulled the crumpled paper out of his pocket.

He was in Hué on combined business and pleasure. This particular business was a matter of interest to a special branch of Headquarters. It had taken him a month to get himself transferred from SF Logistics HQ to HQ in Saigon. After a week in Hué, he now had a few days of R & R, which Ivan told himself were richly deserved, as well as the new silver bird on his shoulder. He frowned. The letter was the worst prank ever pulled on him. Did Dave think he would for one minute swallow that bullshit? He had been looking forward to Devorian's arrival in Hué and was lucky after some maneuvering to be here at the right time to greet Jim's arrival. Ivan went into the dining room, his mind in a whirl. He would order a good French wine. It was a perfect night to get drunk. He'd see Devorian tomorrow as soon as he landed and get the real scoop on the letter in his pocket.

Carrying his glass of scotch, he picked a

table by a window and was about to sit down
when he noticed a major coming into the dining
room. Jim Devorian was walking toward him,
his mouth turned up in the familiar grin. Jim was
saying, "Hey ol' man, gottcha covered! What
are you doing in this crummy hellhole by the
Perfume River?"

Ivan clapped him on the back. "Same thing
you're doing, you ol' bastard!"

"I can think of a few better monikers, but I
suppose I'd better start with colonel." Jim
laughed, wringing his friend's hand.

Ivan grimaced. "That's as good an insult as
any in this Goddam war." He called the waiter to
bring another drink for Devorian. "You're a day
early. When did you get in? Might as well celebrate your arrival in this capital of the world."
He looked inquiringly at Devorian. They both
started to speak at once and stopped, waiting for
the other. Again they both began together.

Now they were chuckling, and Jim said, "Go
ahead. Rank first."

"Are you and Kate married like Dave says or
is it some kind of joke?"

Jim looked at him straight in the eye. "No,
it's no joke. It's true, a surprise to both Kate and
me. I'm so happy it scares me. Are you going to
wish us well?"

"Of course, lucky dog! Congratulations!"
Ivan attempted a light tone. "Here I've been
refused by the redheaded-one for years, and suddenly she's Mrs. Devorian. No really, I'm damn
glad for both of you. Must think of a wedding
present for my two best friends. Here's to your
50th wedding anniversary!" He raised his glass
and gulped it down.

Devorian was relieved to be past the
encounter, wondering what Ivan was thinking
behind his words of unmistakable bravado. He
had lost Kate and that was the end of it. And Jim
was sure they would still be buddies, the three of
them. Nothing could change that. He asked

aloud, "Is anything different since the last time I saw the Perfume River?"

"Not a Goddamn thing," answered Ivan. "It still smells, and I'm talking about the whole shit war." The two men lingered over dinner, catching up on happenings since the last time they were together.

"Tell me. What does Westy have in mind for the next move?" Jim asked.

Ivan finished his wine. "Who knows? Khesanh is still a waste of good men, and that includes the Bru Tribes, poor slobs. Nobody in the Pentagon's even heard of what happened to our camp over there."

"Everybody in SF has heard about it." Jim's tone was somber. They talked a little longer and decided to hit the sack early for different reasons. Ivan wanted to reread Dave's letter. Jim was tired after his flight from Travis. He didn't want to stay awake half the night, so he downed a Thirty-Three beer before leaving the Club. Outside he looked up, thinking the stars seemed extra bright. What time was it in Germany? Did Kate have his roses? He swore.

The next morning Jim and Ivan met again for breakfast at the Club. Jim had had only one day in Hué on his first tour, and Ivan thought it was time his friend saw some of the city's sights, starting with the Imperial Palace Museum. The exhibits were so interesting that Jim was impressed. His enthusiasm faded, however, as he followed Ivan into room after room of ancient artifacts—pottery decorated with gold inlay, jeweled combs, terra cotta statues, intricate screens and ivory fans—all of them with intriguing Vietnamese labels. Ivan charged ahead, calling over his shoulder, "Come on in this room, Jim. You've got to look at these weapons. They're handsome!"

He was warming to his subject and Jim interrupted him. "Jesus! Have a heart! I'm getting hungry. Where can we find some elephant-sized steaks?"

"Ha," said Ivan. "You think I don't know. Follow me."

"I'll believe it when I see 'em. Here's a dollar says you won't find a damn thing but doggie hamburger."

"Stay here long enough and you forget the difference." As it turned out, a trishaw took them to the side street Ivan remembered, but a shoe repair now occupied it, bicycle repair, second-hand shops, other enterprises—and not a trace of former location. "When old Hué changes, it's a bad sign," Ivan said and thought to himself, "always shifting sand, never solid ground." He wondered where he'd heard those words. At somebody's funeral? He had a sudden fervent wish to be free of the stinking war and his whole past stinking life. He muttered, "First damn thing I know, pictures of my childhood will be floating in front of my eyes." Jim caught a word or two and looked at his friend inquiringly, but Ivan said, "Hell, let's get back and play tennis until we forget that life is really shit."

"Good idea," Jim said soberly. They were both thinking of Kate.

The next day, word came that Devorian's assignment was changed to B Company Tactical Operation Center in Canh Lang. Ivan went back to Saigon. They were both elsewhere during the murderous communist takeover of Hué on January 31, 1968, when the TET Offensive officially began. In just a month, many of its beautiful temples and government buildings were destroyed and thousands of its inhabitants including women and children killed in a brutal bloodbath.

The TET Offensive was taking a terrible toll all over South Vietnam and there was a serious shortage of Special Forces. February 2, 1968 Ivan and Jim discovered they were both going to To Canh, a small Special Forces "A"-camp near the Laos border, on the same helicopter. Before

boarding they had a few minutes. "You know
what we're gonna' find—too few old timers
who know the score." Ivan scowled. "I've been
to more of these border camps than you would
believe. Same story everywhere."

"Yeah," Jim agreed, "too many newcomers
need on-the-spot training." The chopper was
warming up. Jim shouted above the noise of
rotor blades, "We won't have time to get 'em
ready. Too many hot spots all over the place."

Ivan nodded. They climbed aboard with
three Special Forces NCOs, fastened on their
gear, gave the pilot the high sign and the chopper took off. Conversation was impossible. It
didn't matter. Their thoughts were far away.

As the chopper began its descent, To Canh
became a small brown clearing in the vast jungle
of intertwined vine and gray green leaves threatening to choke the camp. As the dust whirl of
their landing subsided, Ivan and Jim climbed
down wishing they knew exactly what was hidden under the green umbrella surrounding the
camp and what they could do to fortify this tiny
brown island. Ivan told himself there was no
time to guess what they were up against. They
had to make do with what they found here to
keep out the enemy.

What they found was a solid core of battle-
wise Green Beret NCOs and a new lieutenant
who had just arrived from six months crash
training in Fort Bragg. He had replaced the captain team leader who had left on medical evac to
the States. Most of the Americans were working
night and day on the perimeter defenses.
Sergeant Jablonsky, the demolition expert and
their lone welcoming committee, had been particularly busy planting mines around the outer
perimeter of the camp, not to mention other
places that he now confided to Ivan in the command bunker.

Ivan and Jim looked at each other with the
same thought. The new lieutenant would proba-

bly be useless. Vietnamese troops on leave had
disappeared, and their scouts who were supposed to warn the camp were not reporting in—
presumably prolonging the holiday in their
home villages, or, Ivan thought grimly, defected
to the VC. The few CIDG troops left didn't look
like happy campers. He was sure half of them
would sneak out during the night.

In the communications bunker was a haggard sergeant who assured Ivan in language
unfit for the folks back home that urgent
requests for support had already reached the
proper authorities. So far Vietnamese HQ had
not replied. "How long have you been on the
line?" Ivan asked.

"Too damn long, sir, but I'm taking me pep
pills." Sergeant Jones tried to laugh.

Ivan sent two strongly worded messages
with his name, hoping to reach a Vietnamese
officer he knew personally and trusted. Then he
called his own headquarters with a request for
MIKE reinforcement and sent an update on conditions at the camp. He checked his gun and
ammo. A cold wet blanket of fog hung over
them. It would be difficult to bring in gun ships
and medevac choppers in this weather. Where in
bloody hell were the scouts and the rest of the
strikers? The jungle was silent, listening—wrapping green shadows around the camp.

On his way past the inner defense trenches,
Ivan saw the new lieutenant. "What do you
think, sir?" The lieutenant put down his shovel,
sweating profusely although the temperature
was cool.

"I'm not thinking right now," snapped Ivan,
then seeing the look on the younger man's face,
said quickly, "We'll make it, fella. Just got to go
through a little hell first." Poor guy. Just out of
jump school and probably scared out of his
pants, right in the middle of a war. He added,
"I'm taking over command temporarily and
Major Devorian will have authority in my

absence." The lieutenant's sweat smelled of fear.
Ivan sent him to check in at the command
bunker where Devorian was waiting for the field
telephone to bring some answers. Then Ivan
erased his mind clear of everything that didn't,
couldn't matter and continued his inspection of
camp defenses and guard duty rosters. He and
Jim both knew they were facing almost impossible odds. The almost was what kept them going.
   That night at 2300 hours the big one came. It
was a kind of relief after waiting for the
inevitable. The first wave of Viet Cong breached
the outer defense lines, opening the barbed wire
with mortars and hacking their way through the
barrier of concertinas, dying in a hail of
grenades and charged tripwires.
   Ivan had been in almost continuous contact
with B Camp, and now two gun ships came in
low behind choppers dropping flares. But one of
the gun ships caught in enemy fire went into a
sickening spiral and crashed near the camp,
spreading flames and almost unbearable heat.
The yellow light of flares illuminated the second
and third waves of black-clad VCs advancing
over the bodies of the first, a surreal picture of
hell.
   Sheer numbers engulfed the defending
CIDGs who had survived the first assaults. The
inner camp became a hand-to-hand combat zone
with shadowy figures highlighted in a flickering
lightning and thunderstorm of hand grenades.
Mortars and machine gun fire mingled with
screams of wounded and dying men. The bodies
of VC attackers and CIDG defenders piled just
inside the outer perimeter. The communications
bunker, under heavy attack, was in imminent
danger of being overrun along with the rest of
the camp. Ivan could get no response from
Sergeant Jones.
   A MIKE Force had arrived and was doing a
good job of clearing the area around the northeast tower. Ivan knew they couldn't hold out for-

ever and decided it was time to evacuate the
camp through the northeast corridor.

Crouched low behind a line of sandbags, Jim
ran toward the communications bunker, hoping
to bring out Sergeant Jones. Ivan followed. The
bottom of the trench was slippery and Ivan
stumbled over an SF who had fallen in a bloody
heap. He grabbed the man under what was left of
his arms and dragged him toward the northeast
corner of the camp.

Ahead of him, another explosion gave way
to an eerie silence. A mortar shell had exploded
inches from Devorian's feet. In the long brief
instant before eternity, Jim thought a buddy in
the Park Hotel had blown up the door of his
room—too heavy a charge for a joke. The door
was splintering and fragments fell, turning crazi-
ly—twisted, tired firecrackers in slow, slow
motion.

"Holy Christ! Where are the skin ships?"
Ivan shouted and shifted his unconscious burden
onto his back. He called to Jim but there was no
answer. He thought he heard a faint whirring
sound. In the distance medevac choppers were
coming in low. Could they possibly make it
through the cloud cover?

A flare lit up the ground, but before it blos-
somed there was a deafening explosion. Ivan
heard a sound like empty bottles crashing on a
tin roof below a party in the Park Hotel. Glass
was shattering around him—or was it Zeke—
hanging Shaky Jake by his heels out of a third
story window in the Park Hotel. "DON'T LET
HIM DROP WITHOUT A CHUTE!" he
screamed soundlessly and drifted off into silence
as a surge of air took him up in a sling to one of
three hovering choppers.

Flares lit up bedlam, heroism, and bloody
death as the helicopter carrying Ivan and other
wounded wheeled away. Red clouds faded to
thin wisps of smoke above the jungle brooding
in darkness below. To Canh was a small engage-

ment. There was no mention of it in stateside
newspapers.

Kate found it hard to concentrate.
Sometimes her third graders looked at her
strangely, and she realized she'd added 1 and 1
and got 3. She longed for a letter from Jim. Days
had gone by without mail from him. According
to returning Special Forces, Vietnam was infi-
nitely worse than casualty figures or visiting
congressmen reported.

Peter was back in the States, seeing old
friends, headed for duty in the Pentagon,
"punching his ticket" on the way to a star. His
last letter had described a busy social calendar.
Kate let time go by before she answered.

Ivan woke up in a field hospital. A nurse was
bending over him, but her face kept fading in
and out. "You're going to be OK, Colonel
Herrick," she was saying.

Later when he woke up again, he didn't
remember her voice but his legs were hurting
fiercely. "God! Am I going to lose my damn
legs?"

He must have said it out loud because the
medic standing by his bed answered, "No, I
don't think so, Colonel. Looks like you'll be in
good shape. Soon as we get you fixed up a little
better, we'll send you in to Saigon. Right now
you're getting a shot for the pain. It'll ease off."

Why are all army nurses named Elsie?
Devilish legs! Kind, nice Elsie. Where's
Devorian? Where is Devonian? What the hell—
! He wanted desperately—longed for Kate. Who
was Kate? Elsie? Mira. Poor Mira. The new
lieutenant. I never got his name. Ivan shuddered.
His mind chugged along, a train constantly
changing tracks. It was a big effort and he was
very tired. He thought he would like to discuss
this hellish situation with Kate. She would make
sense out of it one way or another. But he could-
n't remember her face and slipped under into a
black place—without dreams, without shape.

People moved around him; other wounded were brought in, some already dead or dying; but he was unaware, deep in his own darkness.

CHAPTER FIFTEEN

In mid-February the news of Devorian's death reached Headquarters Company in Flint Kaserne. When the Chaplain was found in his quarters, his heart sank. Of all his duties, this was the hardest. He put on a heavy sweater against the late afternoon wind chill, and said a prayer for guidance. Then he drove in the Kaserne gate, around the quadrangle and down the hill to Kate's quarters. Kate came to the door, looked at his face and knew. She had always known. He took her hands, trying to comfort her, but she was white stone, icy cold, sagging against the door.

"No, no—no—." Her voice was hard. "Please go away and leave me. I've got to be alone." She closed the door, and he heard steps, slow steps becoming faster, farther and farther down the entrance hall.

When did I know? Kate was clinging to details. Was it when he put his gear by the door? Said goodbye? No, when? Yes, that's it—yes— when the first roses came—that funeral smell like boxwood, only sweeter. She was gagging and realized she was leaning on the hall table where she had put the vase of roses that morning. The buds were not going to open. The smell of their dying was swelling in the back of her mouth. She groped along the wall into the kitchen, around the roughness of the cupboard, felt her way by the wooden table top, around a chair to the sink and splashed cold water on her face, shivering. The smell of dead roses was a suffocating cloud, surrounding, pursuing her as she walked.

Outside, Dave and Helen had come to see if they could help. They looked at each other. They were both crying. "What can we do?" asked Helen.

"I think she needs time, honey. Later." They waited a few minutes, heard steps in the hallway.

Kate seemed to be pacing back and forth, back
and forth. They consulted and decided to go
home and call a council of friends, the ones who
really cared for each other. They all agreed Hunk
should try again. Angel begged off saying she
couldn't possibly stand all that sadness. It didn't
occur to her that no one, including Hunk, had
asked her to go. In fact he looked relieved. An
hour later he went to Kate's quarters, and when
she heard his voice she opened the door.

"Katie love," he began, "can't somebody
just stay with you for a little while? We don't
want you to be alone."

Hunk was one of Jim's best friends, and she
couldn't turn him away. She put her hand on his
arm, keeping her composure with a superhuman
effort. "What are we going to do, Hunk? What
will we ever do?" She choked and finally broke
into tears.

"Goddamn shit war!" he muttered, turning
on the hall light. They went inside past drooping
red roses on the hall table, talked for an hour,
and when he left she was quieter. No one ever
knew what they said or where her car went for
the rest of the weekend. Hunk returned to the
group at Dave's and told them it was best to let
Kate face it now rather than later. "When she's
ready" His voice trailed off. Helen moved close
to Dave. He was waiting for orders to Vietnam
any day. They tried not to look at each other
because it was on all their faces. Devorian was
gone. Who would be next? Dave poured another drink for everyone. It didn't help but they
drank it anyway.

The phone rang in Kate's quarters. At first
she wasn't going to answer it but after the fourth
ring she picked up the receiver. She heard a few
seconds of static, and then a voice said clearly,
"This is Jim's father, Kate. It is Kate I'm speaking to, isn't it?"

She tried to breathe and said, "Yes, this is
your son's wife."

The voice said, "You have heard."

"Yes," she answered, unable to summon more words.

Another voice came on, Jim's mother. "What can I say to you?" Now they were all three crying. She continued, "—except we love you. Will you come and be with us for the service when Jim comes home?"

With an effort, Kate steadied her voice. "I'm so new to the family. Maybe it's better if I come later and let you be alone together for this time. Where will it be?"

Mr. Devorian answered, "We'll make arrangements for a service in Arlington Cemetery, if that's all right with you. We don't have a date yet. Of course you are the one to make the final decision. We will wait for your approval."

"Please let me think about it." Kate was close to breaking. "I'll call you as soon as I can decide what to do. You have my love. I'll come when I can."

She hung up the phone and tried to think. She knew she could have time off, but to be with Jim's family whom she'd never seen before would be very difficult for all of them at the funeral. Tears flowed down on her clenched fists; "I want to be alone the first time I go to his grave, all alone."

It was late Sunday afternoon, after one of those wintry days when heavy clouds hid the Blomberg, and, as sometimes happened, the sky suddenly opened to focus a piercing beam of sunlight on the Hohemunde south across the Austrian border. She wished it would somehow lighten the murkiness in her mind. But there was no hope of such intervention. Anyway the sudden light in the south would last only a few seconds and always presaged a blizzard when snow fell for days.

Sunday night Jane came over, stamping the snow off her boots on the doorstep. Jane was plump, a warm-hearted, freckle-faced young woman whose classroom was little short of bedlam, but the children were never bored. In her company it was hard to stay dismal. She was apt to point out a wart on her nose.

Jane had brought a pizza and after hugging and kissing Kate, she swooped into the kitchen to put on the coffee pot, keeping up a running conversation. While they were eating, Jane asked when she was leaving for the States. "I'm not going to the funeral," Kate told her.

"Why not?" Jane looked puzzled.

Kate tried to put it into words. "It would be hard for us to comfort each other now. They need time to deal with this without having to meet a complete stranger." She paused, collecting herself. Jane opened her mouth and closed it. Kate went on. "And I want to go to his grave alone the first time." Tears rolled down her face. Jane put her arms around her friend, crying with her.

Finally Jane shook herself. "Listen up, kid! We're running out of my handkerchief. You're going to go on living, believe it or not! I'll hang in there with you and so will the rest of our pals. Come on, now. I'm taking you to Zantl's for dinner tomorrow night complete with a tall beer whether or not you feel like going. Be ready in your best bib and tucker at 6:30 sharp." She picked up her coat and slung it around her shoulders. "Gotta get some shuteye before facing the little dears tomorrow. Monday is always a mess."

The days came and went in dreary procession and after the roses and Jim's letters stopped coming, Kate found she could not grieve all the time. School days were the easiest because she had little time to think beyond Kevin's inability to remember his boots and Susie's problem with multiplication. Weekends and evenings the SFs, Jane and other teachers rallied around and filled some of her hours, talking, venturing small jokes, telling the latest gossip about the Back Door Club, although its members were not generally known except by hearsay. Trading house keys could turn into a dangerous sport.

Sometimes she wished they would all go away and leave her alone. Jane seemed to be always around, a mixed blessing. One night she came in pulling off her coat, ready to launch into stories about old times when they shared an apartment over the Class VI store. There was no way to send her off without hurting her feelings and after all, Jane was just being kind. Kate sighed.

Without preamble, Jane began. "Remember when George and Al used to stop by for a cup of coffee and some conversation after work and one night they stayed longer than usual spinning jokes? It was getting late and Al's wife was on the phone." Kate let her mind go blank. In a way it was soothing just to let the words roll over her. Jane warmed to her story, imitating the wife's voice. 'Is Al over there with you? He hasn't come home for dinner.'" Jane paused for effect. "'Oh, that's all right as long as he's with you girls. Tell him not to hurry.' And Kate, remember you said, 'Damn, Jane! We ought to wear more eyeshadow and some really devastating wigs!' Remember? And I said, 'Why not start our own Back Door Club?'" Kate managed a small giggle, and the very effort was good medicine.

Jane's stories and the most harmless bits of gossip gave Kate something to write Ivan along with accounts of her own days. He was not famous for listening patiently to anecdotes about school. Just now he was mostly interested in what the doctors at Walter Reed had to say, and they were telling him how lucky he was to come out of surgery with only a slight limp. "Hell!" he growled, "Who's gonna limp!" He worked grimly at his therapy with the aid of a few drinks smuggled in on the side to keep him limber.

Kate kept postponing decisions. Should she stay overseas with the most happy and sad memories of her life, or what would make better sense? Finally, Jane suggested they take an Easter vacation trip to Greece and try to sort it out away from familiar surroundings, put things in perspective. "Maybe, like the ancient Greeks, you'll find an answer in Delphi!" Kate didn't care one way or the other, so it was easy to acquiesce.

The four days before Good Friday were busy for all the teachers. Kate's third graders made Easter baskets and colored eggs. On Wednesday they wrote a poem together for cards to take home. Kate was not sleeping well, but Thursday night she fought to keep awake because she still hadn't packed her bag for the trip. Their flight left from Munich the next morning. Jane had been ready since Monday. In fact, that day, disregarding the curriculum, she had started her fourth graders on an ambitious unit about Greece. By the last day before vacation, her class could count to ten in Greek, had learned a song and dance to go with it and were labeling maps with the names of major Greek cities.

Kate was only vaguely aware of these goings on and totally disinterested in the coming trip. If possible she would have been happy to back out. But the morning of their departure she tried not to dampen Jane's enthusiasm. It wasn't necessary for Kate to talk on the way to Munich. She was very good at listening or not listening to Jane's running commentary on the geography of Greece.

CHAPTER SIXTEEN

Jane's enthusiasm was contagious. By the time they stepped off the plane into the crowded uproar of Athens International Airport, Kate began to feel some excitement in the bustle of tourists from all over the world milling around the baggage claim room. She heard snatches of English, French, and German, and local guides held up signs to herd tourists into their groups. Kate discovered she was smiling. Jane pulled her along. "Come on, Kate! We have to grab a cab before the rest of this mob takes 'em all!"

They found their baggage and reached the waiting line of taxis. It was almost noon. None of the drivers seemed anxious for a fare and some of the cabs left empty, their drivers heading for the Kaffinéo or home, depending on their need for an afternoon nap. Finally a policeman held out his hand and a cab pulled over to the curb.

Their hotel was small, unpretentious, and located on a side street near the Plaka. They left their bags unopened in their room, picked up some travel brochures at the entrance, and walked until they found a taverna with tables in the garden. Most Athenians had already eaten their noon meal, and the tables were empty around them. An occasional whiff of incense from a chapel on the corner reached them, mingling with the aroma of spanakopita and stuffed peppers on their plates. Jane leafed through the travel brochures. "The first place we want to see is the Acropolis. Have we got time today? Do you think it will be open for tourists on Good Friday?"

"Don't know," said Kate, signaling the proprietor for the check. "Anyway, this year Orthodox Easter is a week later than ours, so it isn't Good Friday." They decided to go back to the hotel and find the owner who spoke English. Mr. Philicatos called his teenage son, Stefanos, a

gangly, bright-eyed boy who offered to take
them to the Acropolis himself.

"You can see it from here." Stefanos
motioned Kate and Jane to follow him to the
street. He pointed. There it was above the city.
They could even see the outline of the
Parthenon. Kate was relieved to find that for
once Jane was too excited to say a word.

By the time a bus had taken them to the
Acropolis, it was mid-afternoon and the shadows began to lengthen. They sat propped up in
the sun among the broken marbles inside the
entrance, while Stefanos scampered nearby,
impatient to give them his version of a guided
tour. Even in the vast accumulation of history
around her, Kate found no relief from her grief.
If only Jim were here with her. She opened the
guidebook but the words seemed unimportant.
She pretended to read, thinking. Just a little over
a month ago, Jim was alive. She tried to concentrate on the guidebook. Centuries ago, Athenians
must have seen war as a necessary part of life.
How was that possible? How did they cope with
so much death?

Jane broke in, laughing. "Look at those
tourists, will you! Would you want any of those
rich old bald-headed men? I'm glad I'm single!"
She looked suddenly stricken. "Sorry, Kate! I
have a big mouth! Just tell me to shut up."

"Come off it, Jane! You don't have to step
around me like I'm made of eggshells," which
sounded irritable. Kate tried to make amends.
"Don't mind me. I know I'm not much fun to be
around. How do you put up with me?"

"It's easy," smiled Jane. "Tomorrow let's
take a bus tour that goes to Delphi and some
wonderful places in the Peloponnese. It'll take
about six days. We have time, and I've always
wanted to see where the oracle sat on her tripod
and foretold the future. We need some advice."

"All right," said Kate. "But the oracle spoke
in riddles, so we won't be any better off than

before."

"It'll be fun," enthused Jane. Kate looked dubious but in spite of herself felt a spark of interest. Did Jane really believe there would be an oracle in Delphi?

Stefanos was eagerly waiting for them so they followed him through the ruins. He was quite knowledgeable about the history of the Acropolis and other antique sites he pointed out in the city below them. Kate began to feel time stretching into the past under her feet. So much had happened here, both triumph and tragedy. Her sorrow was walking among ghosts.

Back at the hotel, they gave Stefanos a tip in American dollars, which made his face break into a delighted grin. "Ef haristo, POLI!" he exclaimed, forgetting to speak English.

Jane called the tourist agency to book their tour. They had time to unpack and sort out what they would take along before going back to the taverna where they had eaten lunch. Evening outings begin late for Athenians, and Jane and Kate were almost finished before locals from the neighborhood began to fill empty tables. At about the same time, strains of bouzouki music drifted over the garden. The musicians quickly identified Kate and Jane as foreigners and clustered around their table. Jane wanted to stay, but the mournful notes of bouzouki songs were making Kate miserable. However, she kept her face set in a smile. They left amid a clatter of dishes and conversations, before plentiful glasses of wine had taken effect among the people around them. Outside the tavern, they could still hear loud laughter and chatter.

The tour departed early the next morning. Kate closed her eyes as the bus rolled through the countryside. The sun was shining on her side, and the warmth was pleasantly relaxing. Soon their guide's voice faded, and she slept until they reached the famous Castalian Spring near Delphi. Kate was the last to climb off the bus. Jane grabbed her arm. "Come on! If you're going to ask the oracle anything, you have to be sprinkled with water from this spring."

"And then do I have to sacrifice a goat?"

"Naw, we'll skip that part." Jane hoped no one was listening. She bent low, almost falling into the trickle of water, cupped some drops in her hand, and sprinkled them on Kate's hair. "Now you're ready for the Pythia. Just ask her if you should stay in Germany."

"Really, Jane. You must be crazy. Where do you think we're going to find a damn oracle?"

Jane sounded confident. "You'll see." The other passengers were boarding the bus and they followed.

Kate noticed an American couple eyeing them strangely. She cringed. Next thing I know, a white coat will come for us with a butterfly net!

Their tour group ate lunch in a restaurant high on a ridge above Delphi where they could catch glimpses of the dark blue Gulf of Corinth below wooded slopes. A dessert of rich, sugary plums in yogurt sent the group off to see the temple ruins and statues in a receptive mood. But Jane was itchy. Sorely testing the guide's patience, she kept asking him when they could stop in town for some shopping. Back on the bus, he looked at his watch, picked up the microphone and announced, "You have one hour for shopping." His face showed disapproval. The bus traveled downhill and stopped in the middle of a street with rows of souvenir shops on both sides.

Jane hopped off first, dragging Kate along with her. She had seen what she was looking for, a small building with a large hideous eye painted on the front and a big sign above it, "THE ORACLE". Kate took one look and pulled back. "NO! No, and again, NO. I'm not going in there for all the tea in China! You go if you want to. I'll wait half an hour and then call the police."

All Jane's pleading did nothing to change her mind.

"Oh well, there'll be another day." Jane was disappointed but philosophical.

"Not if I can help it!" Kate announced with set chin, resolving to be on her guard against any more rash ideas.

As the trip progressed, the busload of tourists settled into a routine of sightseeing among more antiquities than they could remember, collecting stacks of postcards, maps, and guides to help them sort it all out when they were back home. Seated on the top row of the great stadium in Epidaurus, Kate heard clearly the whispered words of the tour guide far below in the center of the field. The words, first voiced by an ancient philosopher, sounded irrelevant. Later, she trudged up a deep-rutted chariot road through the Lion Gate at Mycenae, stood at the runners' finish line in Olympia, and thought how short and insignificant the track seemed. What would Jim have said?

The sights finally became a blur in Kate's mind, dimly remembered myths with no meaning. At the end of the journey, the only place she could recall in detail was Mistra where she found an answer of sorts. She did not recognize it then for a sign of the future.

While their bus journeyed toward this medieval enclave, the guide told them why it was important in the long history of Greece. Most of his group had never heard of it. The tour was almost over and it took his best efforts to keep them awake.   Mistra was an oddity among the ancient ruins they had seen, dating back only to the 13th Century. Located four miles west of Sparta through olive groves, its summit rose steeply more than two thousand feet above the plain to the ruins of a Frankish castle and the remains of a town and monasteries of the Byzantine Period.

The guide's introduction ended and the bus

stopped. Again, its passengers stepped out, looking with dismay at the rough, narrow paths wandering upward over rocks. They wound around thick bushes, Byzantine churches, monasteries, a mosque, and the remaining stones of villas and a palace, only the tops partly visible from below.

Kate chose a path that looked level while most of the others, including Jane, followed the guide in another direction. Their voices faded away rapidly. Soon the only sound Kate heard was the crunch of her sandals on the ground. She came to diverging paths and chose the one going down, but just around the curve, it twisted upward along the edge of the mountain. Again she came to a fork, selected the down slope, only to meet a sudden upward curve. A third time the path drew her one way then abruptly turned her around.

She sat down on a boulder to rest and tried to decipher the old wooden signs in Cyrillic pointing down two paths ahead of her, separated by a doorway overgrown with weeds. The door seemed to lead to a former church, judging by fragments of religious painting under the portico. Nothing was left of the church except the doorframe standing alone in dense undergrowth. Bees buzzed in a clump of tiny yellow wild flowers beside her feet. Behind and below her was a main road, but the bus was not in sight. She felt comforted by soft sounds of nature around her, and her muscles relaxed.

After a few minutes, Kate walked farther along the path she had chosen and came upon a small, well-tended courtyard. At the near end was a building with an open door. Inside a narrow whitewashed room, she saw the shadowy figure of a nun and a wooden bench, which held some religious objects. The nun smiled and beckoned her in, pointing to the items obviously for sale. Something about the gentle breeze against her skin, the welcoming, silent nun, and her frame of mind made Kate pick up a small icon from the bench. It was only two inches high and about three inches long when its three panels were unfolded, gilded, with plain brown wood showing through the gold. Pasted on the center panel was the paper picture of a dark-eyed Christ, solemn, looking out at the world, perhaps at her?

Kate gave the nun a few drachmas and the nun wrapped the icon carefully in old newspaper. Kate noticed she had laid a slip of paper inside with Cyrillic writing on it. The nun crossed herself and put a blessing on Kate's forehead, handing her the small package. Slipping it into her pocket, Kate found her way back to the bus, having missed all the tourist sites of Mistra, but more at peace than she had been for a long time.

Back in Athens the next day, Kate repacked her bag for the trip home to Bad Tölz. She found the small paper-wrapped parcel tucked in one of her shoes and opened it. There was the icon and the strip of paper with printed Greek words. Like a Chinese fortune cookie, she thought. Curious to know what it said, she showed it to the hotel proprietor. Mr. Philicatos translated, "Bless you, my child. You will travel to faraway shores and return not dead. By the water you will find God's peace." He saw that she was taking the message seriously and added, "It is like the oracle, spoken in riddles. The words can mean whatever you want them to mean. I am sure they are good words for you." Kate did not tell Jane about the small piece of paper, but for some reason she did not throw it away.

CHAPTER SEVENTEEN

Back home after their vacation, Kate's sleepless nights returned. Spring was unusually late even for the Alps, and cold rains enveloping Upper Bavaria did nothing to cheer her mood. One dark afternoon she came home from school to her apartment, unlocked the door and the long shadows of the empty hallway opened in front of her. They seemed to say, "Remember—remember-. It will never be the same." She made her decision as she closed the door behind her and laid a stack of school papers on the hall table. She would change everything about her life, resign in June and go back to Wyoming, rather than face the places she and Jim had been together any longer.

When her friends heard about it, they were alarmed. "Are you sure that's what you really want to do?" Jane asked. Kate seemed to be regaining her normal spirit, but she still had dark circles under her eyes and she was too thin— probably not eating enough. Jane added, "Maybe you should wait a little longer, give yourself more time. You know, Katie, life has a way of coming out all right if we don't force the issue. Sorry to sound so philosophical but it does really work that way. Don't be in a hurry."

"You might be right. Maybe. But I have to make a move, any kind of a move. Can't just sit down and wait for things to be better. Maybe I should get out of teaching, start raising sheep— something, just so it's different." Seeing Jane's horrified expression, Kate burst out laughing. "Don't worry. No sheep! I've been on my own a long time, and I'll be all right."

After school and on weekends Kate began sorting through her possessions, deciding what to take with her and what to give away or sell. The difficulty was she had no idea where her final destination would be. She had said Wyoming, but her childhood home was totally

different from her life in Europe, no opera, art
museums, nor anything she loved about living
overseas. She would be adding culture shock to
her present misery. On the other hand, open
empty spaces might be good medicine.

The Meissen plates found in an antique shop
in Munich and her French clock would not fit
into the old houses in her little western town.
But pewter plates would be right at home. And
what about the antique wooden cupboards, now
scarce and worth a lot of money in Germany?
Would they even survive the trip across the
Atlantic?

"Why did I collect all this stuff?" Kate asked
Jane in despair one afternoon. "I came over here
with two foot lockers, and look how they've
grown." Kate was sitting on the floor trying to
pull out a big flat carton wedged under her bed.
"I have no idea what's in this damn box. Might
as well wait 'til one of the guys comes along and
hauls it out."

"Leave it for the packers is my advice. They
do everything. Why bother except for your
pearls and emeralds!" Jane started for the
kitchen. "C'mon. I'll make us some ham sand-
wiches and we'll have a beer if you've got any
in the fridge."

While they were eating, Kate thought of
another problem. "You know what else is going
to take a lot of time and trouble? I've got to sell
my old car or leave it on a junk heap. It's not
worth taking home."

"What the heck! Let's call it a day." Jane
took her last bite and started for the door. On the
way out she remembered something. "Kate,
don't lie awake over this, but when the Prestons
packed out, they had to get a certificate saying
their old wooden table from the Munich flea
market was fumigated and free from wood-
worms."

"Oh great!" Kate groaned. Before she could
ask any questions, Jane was gone. Kate began to

take books out of a quartermaster bookcase and pile them on the dining room table, thinking aloud. "I'm certainly going to keep all the guide-books and museum catalogs." The stacks of books grew. She could not find anything she wanted to throw away. Would her weight allowance cover all of them? Finally Kate gave up in disgust and put all the books back on the shelves.

The next day she wrote Connie, her college roommate, saying she would be coming to the States in June. If convenient, she'd like to spend a few days with her before visiting Jim's parents on Long Island. An answer came back by return mail telling Kate to come and stay as long as possible. Connie concluded, "It's been too many years since we've seen each other. I want you to meet my husband. You'll like him."

I hope so, thought Kate. Anyway, I'll need some time to get my bearings before meeting the Devorians.

The last day of school arrived. The children had gone home with their report cards, and Kate sat at her desk emptying drawers. The wastebasket overflowed. Jane passed Kate's open door and caught a glimpse of her head down on the desk. She came back and stepped inside the door. "Can I help? My stuff's all cleared out."

Kate raised her head. "My household goods are going to be packed tomorrow. Do you think it's too late to back out? I don't know if I'm ready to go. It's such a big change in my life. I should have stayed here for part of the summer to get used to the idea of leaving. Oh, Jane. I'm so tired!"

Jane decided it wouldn't do to sympathize. "Now Kate, you've been through all this before. Cut loose and get it over with! Here, I'll help you." She found a big trash bag and emptied the wastebasket.

Early the next morning the packers' truck stopped in front of Kate's quarters. Panic clutched her throat. Maybe if she didn't open the door, they'd go away. She willed herself to let them in, and the three German packers went to work, hauling in what seemed to be tons of heavy cardboard boxes and stacks of wrapping paper.

By the end of the day they had finished; she signed several forms, and they drove away with all her possessions except hand baggage she would take with her. She had sold her car to a GI with the warning that he should watch for rust from the salt on winter roads. It was somehow a relief to have everything gone. There was no way now to change her mind. She was in a state of hibernation where nothing mattered. Her third graders, men in the 10th who had worked with Jim and their families, other teachers, and close German friends all kept her occupied during her few remaining days, giving Kate few moments to regret her decision.

The farewell parties were over, rather subdued considering the circumstances. The day of Kate's departure, Hunk and Angel drove her to the Munich airport, while Jane and other friends followed in their cars. They thrust flowers and candy in her arms at the gate, leaving her no time for anything at the last minute except goodbyes.

As her plane circled, turning away from Flughafen Riem on the way to New York, Kate watched south and caught a glimpse of the church in Holzkirchen, beyond it, Bad Tölz inside the rim of the Alps. Her eyes were full of tears. What am I doing going so far away from the place I love and where Jim loved me? She thought of some favorite lines by Conrad Aiken, which fit the situation too well. They were not comforting.

"And I myself on a swiftly tilting planet stand before a glass and tie my tie."

Ivan had compared it to T.S. Eliot—"measuring out his life with coffee spoons"—signs of

the time—angst. They had had a long discussion
about it, summed up by Ivan because it was midnight and he was tired and ready to go back to
the BOQ. "Angst is the human condition—all
the time, now and forever amen." And that was
that. As he went out the door, he'd added, "Not
Angsthase meaning coward."

Am I an Angsthase? I should have stayed
and faced the music. Kate knotted her green
scarf, tucking it under her collar, and opened a
magazine trying to focus on an article about
museums in New York City. What about Ivan?
Would they ever spend another evening talking
about nothing—and everything?

CHAPTER EIGHTEEN

When her plane landed at Kennedy it was late afternoon and a rain shower slanted down the windows in sliding paths of air. Damn rain keeps following me! Kate unfastened her seatbelt as the plane taxied into its appointed position. She left the plane reluctantly. It had been a warm cocoon—no wondering if you'd taken the other road, going with the bird—nothing to look at but clouds and an occasional glimpse of the ocean's wrinkled skin below, time streaming behind her—a slowing down. But now she had to go out of the cocoon feeling weak and unready. She hoped Connie was there, but among the people waiting at the gate, she was nowhere to be seen—just unknown faces lighting up, recognizing friends and—lovers—not for her. Kate started down the concourse feeling queasy among hurrying crowds, all with known destinations—homes, waiting cars—. Where am I going? Why? Get your baggage you fool! She set her jaw, straightened and clutched her carry-on tighter. The army had been a kind of cocoon too. It was no use. She looked down a long emptiness of years, and just then Connie appeared, running toward her with open arms.

"Sorry I'm late! The traffic is horrendous around here! How are you, long lost pal?"

"Connie! Thank God! I'm lost all right in this hullabaloo! I'm meant for small towns and wide open spaces."

"I know. New York is kind of intimidating, but it shouldn't bother a world traveler like you. Are you really planning to live in Wyoming?"

"Haven't made up my mind for sure. The crystal ball isn't working too well just now." Ivan flashed into her mind again. They'd had a long conversation about fortunetellers. She remembered the Hungarian music that brought it on. He'd told her a sketchy story about some gypsy with a scar on her face. Her name was

Vera, a beautiful girl who lived with her grandfather in a town on the Danube. Something Ivan
said made her think the old man was a spy—
Russian, maybe.

Baggage was coming in on the conveyor,
and Connie was waiting for an answer, but Kate
couldn't remember the question. "Sorry, Connie.
What did you say? These are mine—the gray
ones."

"They weigh a ton. Are they full of gold
bricks? Never mind. Bill's picking us up at the
exit."

Connie's new husband had been acquired
recently after her messy divorce. He seemed like
a nice guy, and later over dinner, Kate learned
that he'd been an army surgeon at the Frankfurt
U.S. Military Hospital. Now he was in private
practice on Long Island and, judging from their
home, doing very well indeed.

"Why did you get out of the military?" Kate
asked. "I guess the pay isn't very good compared to private practice."

"That too," he answered, "but the incentives
and extra benefits aren't too bad over there.
Mainly, I got tired of constant personnel
changes—in the worst scenarios, mixed-up lab
reports—not that there weren't good medical
personnel over there. It was just difficult sorting
them out before they were assigned elsewhere or
went skiing." He was on his fourth glass of
wine.

They went into the den and Bill poured small
icy glasses of pear schnapps saying, "I don't
bring this stuff out for just anybody, but you'll
know how to knock it back like a true Bavarian."

"Doctor's orders!" Kate felt the warm glow
spreading down her throat. Bill drank, then
excused himself saying he had an operation first
thing in the morning and needed to get a good
night's sleep. The two friends were alone.

Connie studied her glass. "How are you really doing, Kate? This is a big change, but you can

handle it if anybody can. Such a ghastly war. I'm so sorry!"

"Well, I have to pick myself up and make a life somehow—don't know how, but I s'pose it'll work out—try not to be the specter at the ball. Jim's parents and his brother's family live here on Long Island, and I'll spend a few days with them before I fly out to Wyoming. There wasn't much time for him to tell me about them, but they've written me some wonderful letters. I sent them pictures of the wedding and their response was warm, way beyond my expectations. They must be a very close and loving family. I'm nervous about meeting them—without Jim." She folded her lips tight to keep them from trembling.

Connie stared at Kate and shook her head. "I just don't think you ought to go off alone to Wyoming of all places. Why don't you think about living here on the East Coast? Long Island is quieter than the city but close to the bright lights—and me—and Jim's family. Or there's D.C. You'd be near a lot of your overseas friends."

"Can't back out just yet. I'll give my old hometown a try." She took a deep breath and pushed her hair away from her face. "Can always change my mind. Let's talk about you, Connie. Are you happy now, really happy after all the bad times? You deserve a change for the better!"

Connie saw that the answer was important to her friend. Because they were close, she was truthful, more than she had admitted to herself. "My first marriage was a complete fiasco and I'm glad to be out of it. Now Bill—well, Bill was in the military long enough, saw enough torn-up bodies to stress out. Being a surgeon isn't the most relaxing work in the world but he loves it. You probably noticed—he drinks too much sometimes. I didn't realize how much until I married him. Anyhow it's all right.

Everybody has faults and his is under control.
He never drinks when he's working—or driving." She stopped. "Yes, I'm happy. It's better
than living alone. Much better, and Bill is very
good to me. He's really a dear."

Kate chose her words. "Drinking has a way
of magnifying time and, if you think prospects
for a long life aren't good, you drink. It's dirt
cheap in Class VI stores. There's more to it than
that, but let's not talk about it."

She knew for Ivan and many combat veter-
ans it wasn't simple. You build a wall around
memory, never talking about what's inside—to
anybody—but sometimes monsters creep out
from behind the wall—your buddy, the one you
went through boot camp and jump school
with—cut goddam in half right beside you—
dead bodies—or worse, the dying not yet dead,
the smell, the incredible, horrible smell, bloody
dirt, sweat, explosions that almost blow out your
ears—-and now you need a drink re-e-al bad.
But not everyone understands that. She'd heard
worse when men didn't know what they were
saying.

The two women talked for a while about
mutual friends from college days, but Connie
didn't volunteer any information about the
break-up of her first marriage, and Kate didn't
ask about it. Each of them gave the other space,
knowing there would be time if they wanted to
share the details. Kate was thankful Connie did-
n't hover over her like a mother hen. It made it
easier for her to control her emotions.

Finally, Connie took their glasses out to the
kitchen. "Time for bed. I know you're exhausted after that long flight, and tomorrow's another
day." Kate followed her friend to a guest room
upstairs. She fell sound asleep almost as soon as
her head touched the pillow.

They spent the next few days at home, catching up, giving Kate a chance to unwind, and then
they went on a major shopping expedition into

the city. Kate's morale needed a lift and some new clothes seemed to be the answer. Bill met them for dinner in a new French restaurant off 42nd Street. Kate looked at them across the table, smiling. "You've done wonders for me. How can I ever thank you?"

"No need," Bill said. "It's great to have you here. Next time we'll take in some shows. I'm not always as busy as I've been this week. Oh, I know you get along without me very well—especially on shopping trips." He grinned. "What on earth is in all those packages?"

"Not much you'd be interested in," said his wife, winking at Kate.

"I'll have to wear what I bought." Kate looked guilty. "There's no more room in my baggage." Connie was pleased. Her friend was beginning to look and sound more like the Kate she used to know.

Inside, Kate dreaded the next day when Jim's brother was coming for her. She wondered if she was equal to the days she would spend with the Devorian Family. "Just takes gumption!" she told herself sternly.

Late Saturday afternoon Kate's brother-in-law came to pick her up—a soft languid day with an offshore breeze ruffling her long hair as she walked down the steps to meet him. Kate liked him at first sight. George was a younger edition of Jim—the same dark eyes that looked straight at you.

"Welcome to the family, Kate!" He gave her a friendly hug, and she saw a shadow of pity pass over his face. He picked up her two bags and she followed him to the car, waving good-bye to Connie.

The station wagon pulled away from the curb. "We're all anxious about meeting you for the first time, Kate—want to make a good impression on Jim's wife. He had good taste. I can see that!"

His voice was like Jim's but he talked faster,

certainly not the quiet type. Maybe he was as
nervous as she was. She patted his hand, "Thank
you, George. You've said just the right thing
because I'm pretty nervous myself!" and they
talked easily as he wove through five o'clock
traffic.

"I brought Peg and the kids over to mom and
dad's so you could meet the whole shebang at
once. It'll be lively, but we'll go away after dinner and give you a little peace and quiet—time
to get used to the Devorian family."

"I'm looking forward to being part of it—
hoped for a different kind of homecoming." She
took a deep breath controlling a catch in her
voice. "I know how hard it is for all of you—a
stranger instead of Jim coming home."

"You're not a stranger, Kate. Jim wrote
about you in his letters so we think we know you
at least a little." He turned a corner and pointed.
"There's the house, the one with all the rose
bushes in front."

The rest of the grownups were gathered at
the door and greeted Kate warmly, Jim's mother
with tears in her eyes. When George's two eld-
est saw their grandmother crying, they burst into
tears, retreating behind their mother, and the
baby began to shriek, clutching her mother's
legs, adding to the uproar. Kate hastily pulled
out presents—a small huggable teddy bear for
three-year-old Lisa, a mechanical toy truck for
George Jr. and a Bavarian doll dressed in a
Dirndl for Ghada who was six. Seeing these
treasures, the baby stopped in mid-howl; their
grandmother rushed into the kitchen to rescue a
pot of rice, which was about to boil over; and
Peg exclaimed, "What a rousing reception to
this family!"

Kate laughed, giving her attention to the two
oldest children who were still regarding her with
some suspicion. "Did you know that your Uncle
Jim used to call me Little Red Riding Hood?"

"No! Why? You're big!" George, Jr. paid no

attention as his sister jiggled his arm.

"See if you can guess." Kate pushed her hair back.

"I know! Because your hair is kind of red! But Gaby in my kindergarten class has really red hair!"

Ghana was a year older, superior, "There's lots of kinds of red, silly! See, in my crayon box!"

Kate rescued him. "My hair is a funny kind of red." George, Jr. looked grateful, hugging his truck.

Kate's days with the Devorians were emotional, but she did her best. They showed her old photos of Jim as a baby, his high school graduation picture, standing in front of the family restaurant with his father, in college before he left for the army, and a big-framed photo of him in his green beret, which they promised to have copied for her. Finally she asked to see a photo of his first wife. They had evidently put it away but reluctantly brought it out—a wedding picture. The girl looked out at her, dark-eyed and pretty in a white satin dress with a high lace collar and a bouquet of white lilies in her hand. It was painful knowing this girl had had so much more time with Jim and had not prized it—hours and months she longed for. Jim's mother said slowly as if admitting it for the first time, "It was a mistake for both of them. Parents shouldn't pick out life partners for their children. George decided for himself and they're happy, thank God! The old ways don't work here."

Jim's father took Kate's hand. "We're sorry you don't have a grandchild for us. Jim loved you so much."

"So am I." Kate fought back tears. She was relieved when it was time for George and Peg to take her to the airport. So much emotion had made the visit nerve-racking.

In the crowded boarding area at last, she hoped the complete change of new surroundings, nothing to remind her, would force her, challenge her to regain her old independent spirit. But the plane couldn't fly fast enough to keep out the nagging thought that she would regret going so far away from her friends—the ones who really counted like Hunk, Dave and Helen, Ivan.

CHAPTER NINETEEN

When she stepped off the bus in the small western town near her father's old ranch, she was certain she had made a mistake. The place was little more than four corners now with one dreary group of shops, empty dusty windows, and a sign `Old West Mall`. The sky was gray with heat. It was hard to breathe the dry wind.

Her father's cousin took her bags from the driver and hoisted them into the back of his pick-up truck. His hands were knobby and knarled with arthritis. What kind of a life did he have in this Godforsken place? He saw her look of disbelief as she climbed into the truck. "The town's gone downhill since you were here last time. How long is it? Ten years? Small ranches like your father's have almost all been swallowed up. There are two real big ones now, owned by people from outside the state."

"What happened to the engineering company north of town?"

"Gone. Went bankrupt. C'mon, Adie's been cooking all day. There's a big meal waiting for you."

"Oh, Charlie, I told you I'd take you out for supper. But I don't see any eating places, or is that Mom's Kitchen over there? How about that tomorrow?"

"We'll see when tomorrow comes. Adie'll want you to eat at home. Can't beat her apple pie!" The wind was kicking up eddies of dust and the mournful sound of it was the sound of her childhood. The wind followed them into the house, slamming the door behind her.

Adie, a spare woman, smiles wrinkling her face, bustled out of the kitchen, wiping her hands on her apron. Since Kate's last visit Adie's brown hair, pulled back in a knot and streaked with gray, had turned to white and softened the sharp angles of her face. The women hugged each other. "Has it really been ten years

since you were here on your way to California?
You had a college friend with you, I remember,
and you could only spend three days with us.
This time I hope you can stay longer." Kate
started to speak but Adie went on. "Charlie's
sold his hardware store—for next to nothing, so
he's retired and can show you around—down
the valley."

Adie took a breath, and Kate said hastily, "I
don't need to be entertained. Just want a few
days to slow down and get my bearings. It'll be
nice just to be with you."

Adie patted Kate's shoulder. "We're so sorry
this awful thing happened to you. Married so
late and then such bad luck. You know you can
stay here with us as long as you want. Your letter said something about maybe settling down
here. It would please your mother and dad to
know you came back home. But I don't know.
There's not much excitement around here. What
would you do with yourself after living in
Europe so long?"

"To be truthful, Adie, I have no idea. But I'll
think about it and look around while I'm here."
Did Adie have to say so late? Thirties isn't late!

"It would be so nice to have you close by,"
Adie continued wistfully. She went back to the
kitchen, calling back, "Charlie, take Kate's bags
upstairs to the guest room and show her where to
put her things. Suppers on the table in five minutes if you're ready.

Kate followed Charlie upstairs. He was
chuckling. "Adie talks a lot, but she doesn't get
much chance to talk to anybody except me—and
I don't always listen." He set down Kate's bags.
Wind rattled the one window in the room. The
sun was setting brilliantly through a haze of dust
in the lower atmosphere. Charlie went back
downstairs, and Kate looked around the small
bedroom. Hooked rugs disguised part of the bare
wooden floor. A framed Maxfield Parrish print
hung above a chest of drawers, and the Victorian

dresser had a long attached side mirror. Her reflection looked back at her, sad-faced. Deliberately, she smiled. Not much of an improvement, she decided, and ran a comb through her hair. It needed washing. Thank God, there's a bathroom even if it's downstairs. Long ago, the Park Hotel had had bathrooms down the hall. Now she was older and not interested in roughing it.

Charlie and Adies' voices drifted up the open stairway. She remembered they were waiting for her, put on her happy face and went down to supper. The table was loaded with food. It smelled good, but she wasn't hungry. Adie had obviously worked hard and probably stretched her budget to provide this abundance. Not wanting to disappoint her, Kate ate some of everything, asked for a second helping of carrots and finished with a small piece of apple pie. More, she could not manage.

While she helped with the dishes, she listened to Adie's stories of her childhood, bringing back incidents she'd forgotten. It was interesting but the wail of the wind, an unrelenting presence, took her attention away from Adie's words. Finally Kate excused herself, pleading exhaustion. The wind knocked at her bedroom window, an insistent rattle endlessly repeating through restless hours until she fell asleep.

In the morning Charlie drove her to the place where her father's ranch had been. The buildings had all been torn down and fences with NO TRESPASSING signs kept him from driving some miles further where the horse barns were now located. She recognized nothing. Even the distant horizon struck her as unfamiliar. She tried to remember how it looked the last time she had seen it ten years before, but her mind was a blank. I've even lost my childhood, she thought, hiding her dismay from Charlie.

That night she called Dave and Helen in D.C. His tour in Vietnam had been changed to

duty in the Pentagon. "I've been out of touch
here a too long, look like. Can I sponge off you
a few days 'til I think what to do?"

"Come on, Babe!" It was Dave's hearty
voice. "Stay with us as long as you want. Our
house is yours! You know that. You're family,
kid!"

"You sure?"

Helen came on the phone. "Sure? Honey, the
ol' gang is waiting for you! Hurry up! When?
When?"

"I'll let you know. A couple of days." The
quiver in her stomach began to subside and she
slept well that night.

The next evening Ivan called. "What the hell
are you doing out in that Godforsaken place? I
always knew you were crazy!" He repeated all
the reasons D.C. was the center of the uni-
verse—Kennedy Center, concerts, art galleries,
political movers and shakers, and add to that, the
Green Berets she knew. Even those in other units
now stayed in touch near the Pentagon, including out-of-towners who dropped in on their way
to other assignments. His welcome sounded
insulting enough to mean he was genuinely
happy she was coming. She began to feel excited, insisting to herself that his attitude toward
her impending arrival made no difference at all.
But when she looked in the mirror in her bedroom she was smiling—an authentic smile.

Adie wanted some dress material and
Charlie needed to stock up on some lumber to
fix a shed in back of the house, so the next morning they all squeezed into the pick-up and drove
thirty miles to the nearest big town. As a child,
on those rare occasions when she rode there with
her father, Kate thought of Pineville as a metrop-
olis. The name was a misnomer. There were no
pines closer than the foothills of the mountains
on the edge of the horizon. The only trees here
were thin clumps of aspen scattered around the
town. A deep sense of loss came over her,

almost a physical hurt. Pineville was about the
size of Bad Tölz, but what a difference! The
Pineville Elementary School, according to the
date above the entrance, was built in 1929, and
Kate tried to imagine teaching there. She shuddered. The high school was newer, but no matter. She'd soon be far away in D.C. Three inter-
minable days later; Kate was on a bus bound for
Denver and her flight to Washington.

At National Airport Ivan arrived early to
pick her up. He bought a newspaper and started
to read, but even the headlines didn't interest
him. Leaving it on the seat, he went to check
arrival time again. The plane would be a half
hour late. He fumed, impatient. Might as well
have one drink. He'd refused Dave and Helen's
offer to drive over with him. "Just have the bottle open when I bring her back." His fear, well
hidden from himself, was that in the first
moment when she saw him there would be
something in her eyes—the knowledge that he
had survived and Devorian had been a few feet
ahead, and that had made the difference. Ivan
took a deep slug of scotch and it erased the
thought of Devorian from his mind. He sauntered to the arrival gate, determined not to hurry
and there she was, —coming through the gate.
She waved, smiling. Her eyes were clear, the
smile friendly—maybe even a shade more than
friendly.

When they were out of the crush of people
and walking down the concourse, Kate noticed
his limp and the effort he was making to conceal
it. The year had brought them both to the edge of
disaster and neither of them wanted to talk about
what was uppermost in their minds. They found
themselves in awkward silences punctuated by
"How the hell are you? What are your plans?"
and other conversation stoppers and fillers.
Finally they were caught in a traffic jam on the
beltway. Ivan burst into a volley of colorful language; she laughed, and they relaxed into the old

easy relationship, catching up on the news.

Hunk was in D.C. too; Angel's annulment papers were final and he was dating one of the secretaries at the Agency. Ivan's job with the State Department took him around the country to various army training centers and countries overseas. In fact he was leaving for Fort Bragg the next day with a group of Arab officers. "You know what those guys want first after they get out of their own countries?" He swung around a stalled truck. "They want women! I've got to take 'em out bar-crawling tonight."

"What a job!" commiserated Kate. "Must be terrible!" They were laughing as they pulled into Dave and Helen's driveway.

CHAPTER TWENTY

Helen looked at Kate over her cup of coffee, wondering what to say. She had a feeling she could guess what was going on in her friend's mind. It was the morning after Kate's arrival. Dave had left for work and the two were having a late breakfast. Helen waited. The sun shone in the kitchen window and highlighted Kate's red hair. It flashed on Jim's diamond and her fork as she put it down on her plate. "You sure can make good scrambled eggs. They hit the spot!"

"Great!" said Helen. "You look kind of peaked. Here, have some more." Kate shook her head. Helen waited. She can't think how to say it. Finally Helen said aloud, "Is there anything you'd like to do today? Or are you too tired? There's always tomorrow."

"No, today." Kate looked anxious. "Do you care if I go off by myself? I need to go to his grave. I can't put it off a day longer."

Helen quickly nodded. "Of course I don't mind, but are you sure you know how to get there? Suppose I drive you over to the Visitors' Center and we'll find out where it is. I'll drop you off and come back for you whenever you want."

"Oh would you?" Kate looked so grateful Helen had to try hard to keep her voice matter-of-fact. Sympathy at this point was no good.

"Of course!" Helen said again. "We'll get you a pass so you can drive in. Come and go when the notion hits you." She put the dishes in the sink. "I don't want you getting lost. We'll find you a good map of D.C. and before long you'll be tooling around like a native. It takes awhile to learn the shortcuts. In this city it's easy to get stuck on the way to the supermarket—in a parade of some anti-Eskimo group." Kate had to smile.

Helen tried to make conversation as they drove across the city. She saw that Kate's knuck-

les were white from clenching her hands and she
sensed that Kate intended to go to Jim's grave
often and alone. She was concentrating on
remembering the route.

Traffic was snarled so it took longer than
usual to reach the Visitors' Center. Helen waited
while Kate filled out the paperwork for a
Visitor's Pass. They were given a map showing
Jim's grave site and Helen drove on into the
cemetery, flashing her pass at the guard, past
acres of white markers, until they came to the
area shown on the map.

"When do you want me to pick you up?"
asked Helen.

"Is two hours all right?" Kate's voice sounded faint.

"Of course, love. Are you sure you don't
want me to stay?"

"Yes, I'm sure, Helen. Thanks for being so
understanding." Kate got out of the car, clutching the map.

Helen checked her watch. "No problem. It
can't be far from the road, down that path. I'll
see you in two hours." God help her! she
thought, driving away.

Kate trembled. Her knees were weak as she
followed the path down a gradual incline. She
passed a group of people standing around an
open grave. The crack of a 21-gun salute startled
her. She stopped to listen. Taps sounded and the
flag draped on the casket was lifted and present-
ed to a young woman. Other mourners clustered
around the woman and some began going
toward their cars parked on the road Kate had
left.

She found Jim's grave and slumped down on
the ground by his marker, pressing her hands
into the grass. The lawn was too perfect, unlike
the grass and weeds where they had walked up
to the monastery in Sachsenkam, and along the
road under the trees, with marshy bog on one
side and a farmer's field on the other. There had

been a yellow butterfly, even so late in the season. Between ruts made by farmers' wagons and cows' hoof prints were long grasses and small weed flowers with bright blue petals. The air in the late fall had been so clear, not like the oppressive air in Washington. She wiped perspiration and tears from her face. Next time she would bring a bunch of wild flowers for his grave. "Oh, Jim," was all she could whisper.

She sent her mind roving back over their time together, searching for small details that would make it real—Jim looking for a flat stone just the right size and shape to skip over the water, the double rainbow. It had seemed to auger good fortune. She had not been aware of the danger. Had he known, had a dark premonition? She looked around her at rows of markers marching over a berm on her right and down the vale in front of her. All these fallen men lying here together in straight rows, as if marching toward their Maker, no longer as they had fallen in terrible urgency.

She got to her feet by holding on to Jim's marker, caressing it, her suffering like a new grief. For a moment she stood there, then walked further along the path. From the top of a small hill she saw another multitude of graves and two people walking among the markers. The men lying here were alone except for each other, their loved ones scattered among all the states of the Union. She read some of the names as she walked slowly along—Greenberg, Stolz, Martin, Polansky, and Smith. The sound of Taps broke into her thoughts, and she realized she had passed a fork in the path.

Kate was further away than she thought. When she found her way back to Jim's grave, only a half hour passed before she heard a car stopping. She walked up the path to the road and saw Helen. They went home almost in silence until Kate said suddenly, "I should have come for the funeral."

"Don't feel guilty," Helen said. "He isn't here, you know. Just keep him in your heart. That's my advice." Kate nodded, unable to speak.

In bed that night, Helen and Dave talked it over. "What am I going to do with Kate? She's so despondent I'm getting depressed myself. Poor girl!"

"We'd better find her a job," said Dave sleepily. "The sooner the better. Give her something to think about instead of grieving her heart out."

"That's why I married you, darling. You always know what to do. Where shall I start?"

"That's up to you, Doll." Dave rolled over and went to sleep.

"Men!" Helen groaned.

When the morning paper came, Helen and Kate looked through the want ads, but found nothing. They called several suburban school personnel offices and made appointments in two of them where teacher substitutes were needed. Kate kept the appointments without result, except she was asked for recommendations and told there might be openings later.

By the end of the third week Kate had a substitute teacher job in Falls Church and the promise of a regular position as soon as there was an opening. To celebrate, Dave and Helen invited Hunk, his girl friend and Ivan for dinner. Dave brought drinks, and the conversation went from a comparison of apartment prices in the suburbs to trading stories about old timers in the 10th and their present whereabouts. Hunk's friend was looking bored.

"We talk too much about Bad Tölz days," Kate sympathized, "but it was such a special time. I guess the Green Berets—the ones who are still alive—" Her voice quavered and she coughed to cover it, "would all want to go back and re-live that time." She coughed again and took a long swallow of bourbon and ginger. "I must have swallowed a peanut wrong."

Later, as Ivan was leaving he put his arm around her. "You're looking skinny, Babe. Fatten up and you can have me! How about tomorrow for dinner? Can you still dance?"

"Yes," she said.

"Yes what, damn it?"

"Yes, I still do a fantastic minuet! What time?"

"Oh, around 8:00. Thanks for dinner, Helen. You and Dave are not invited."

"Bastard!" said Dave, pretending to punch him in the jaw.

After everybody was gone Helen and Kate were in the kitchen cleaning up. Kate wondered, "Should I go or plead a headache? Am I going to have to drive home from our night out in this unknown maze of traffic because he's drunk?"

"Up to you, Kate. He seems to get around town without any trouble—even seems to be settling down a little since he's been working."

"Now that's really out of character! Well, I'll see how it goes." It was a long time since she'd had a date, although "date" might not be the right word for this particular outing. Ivan was changing, older, with a little gray in his hair, not quite the same confident man she had known in Bad Tölz. Were they both growing up, facing reality, fighting it all the way—and losing? She shook her head, frowning. Let them not turn out to be whiners. Kate looked so forlorn Helen wondered if the happy woman she had known in Bad Tölz was gone forever. At least, Ivan seemed to be able to bring back her old spunk.

The next night Kate took time dressing, getting her hair just right, trying not to think about the one who lived and the one who died because it wasn't right to blame Ivan for living—better to rant against God—or the devil—but no trade-offs. They both deserved to live. But so did thousands of others. She heard the doorbell.

The evening went well. Ivan drank in mod-

eration; they talked about his job; and he offered
to run her around town to look for a car and an
apartment that would be handy to Falls Church
and wouldn't cost a fortune. "I can lend you a
dime or two, Babe, if you need it," were his part-
ing words.

Weeks went by, Kate was settled in an apartment; her household shipment had arrived with
antique German cupboards intact, and her circle
of friends was widening. When Ivan was in
town they were invited to barbecues and dinners
together, went to concerts and art gallery openings, and bets were taken on the date their
engagement would be announced. Kate realized
their relationship was changing, but with the
beginning of school and his frequent absences
she found it easier not to think about it. A vacan-
cy had opened up and she was teaching third
grade, the curriculum and school not too different from her position in Bad Tölz. Many of her
pupils had fathers in the military. Enrollments
were constantly changing. It all seemed quite
familiar.

She and Helen were having lunch during one
of their Saturday shopping trips and Helen
asked, "I'm prying, but what's with you and
Ivan?"

"I'd like to know myself. How can I depend
on someone like Ivan enough to—well, take him
seriously? And if I want to take him seriously,
am I going to be just another in a long line of
dames? —Not what I want to settle for. And he
was Jim's close friend. Will I look at him and
wish he were Jim? That would be horrible!"
Kate was relieved to put it into words.

Helen never thought much before she
opened her mouth but she did her best. "Kate, I
don't know what to say. At least he's a one-
woman-at-a-time man. You know him better
than I do, and although you fight, you do have
fun together. Dave and I fight all the time.
Doesn't mean anything—just makes our sex life

interesting!" She giggled, remembering. "And listen, honey, they all drink. Do you want to stay a widow in black forever?" Kate looked stricken. "Now Kate, don't get shook up! Think future, not past. Live a little! Jim wouldn't want you to be sad forever."

"You're right, but if Jim hadn't been Ivan's friend it would be easier."

"I know. No, —I don't know."

Kate was still mulling over this conversation at home in her apartment when the phone rang. Ivan had just returned from a trip to the Near East. "I'm coming over, Babe. Get out the booze. I'll bring a couple of steaks."

"How do you know I'm not going out? It's Saturday."

"Aren't you waiting for me, crazy girl?"

"Damnation, no!" But he'd already hung up. Thinks he's the only man on earth! She vowed to give him a hard time when he arrived. But a half hour later he offered the package of steaks looking so proud of himself, she only said, "You should be so lucky! I had an invitation to the White House."

"Who do you know over there, the cook?"

She groaned and took the steaks to the kitchen. Following, he found a beer in the refrigerator. "You've really fixed this place up, Babe. Where'd you get that blue glass vase?"

"That's not a vase. It's a Turkish water pipe—an antique—got it in Greece last Easter. I sent you a postcard."

"Oh yeah. Right. Leave me the vase in your will."

"Thanks! That's the nicest thing you've ever said to me! I'm overcome with emotion!"

Steaks were broiling and the aroma was drifting through the apartment while she made a green salad. He opened a bottle of wine and poured two glasses. "You know this is better than the White House!"

"I'll never know. Ignore one engraved invi-

tation and you don't get another, but I do say this
is a darned good steak."

They put the dishes in the sink and settled
into comfortable chairs. He had stashed a flat
package under an end table and now he brought
it out—a recording of *Carmina Burano*.
"Thought you'd like to own this. You guessed
once it was erotic, and you were of course
right." He put the record on and looked at her
thoughtfully as if about to say something more.
The music built
up to loud volume.
"The neighbors!" she shouted.

He turned the volume down an iota and said
tentatively, "A lot of water has gone under the
bridge this year."

"How are you really doing?" Kate asked.
"At least you have an interesting job that takes
you to faraway places."

"I'd rather be jumping out of airplanes, but I
guess I'm lucky." He remembered Devorian
hadn't been lucky and they were both silent as
the music rose to a new shattering crescendo.

The recording came to an end, and Ivan got
up to leave. "I'm sorry, Kate. Never said so but
I am. Ought to tell you. When Jim and I were in
Saigon, he showed me a picture of you under
two rainbows. He had it in his billfold." Ivan
walked toward the door, stopping to pick up a
New Yorker magazine from the coffee table. He
put it back down, careful to line it up with a pile
of other magazines. She waited.

"You know you and I've been friends for a
long time, Babe. Maybe we should be more."

"Maybe," she said without any definable
expression. It was getting late.

Behind the wheel of his car, Ivan asked himself why he'd said all that unmitigated rot. She
was still Devorian's, wasn't she?

In the apartment, Kate put the record on
again while she did the dishes, recovering some
of her old insouciance. If he thinks I'm going to

fall like a ripe tomato, the next in a parade of broads—Mrs. Robert Herrick number what—three? four? Not for Kate O'Brien! Then she heard herself exclaim, "Not for Kate DEVO-RIAN! Stupid idiot, bawling again! Can't I ever stop?"

CHAPTER TWENTY-ONE

Among the occupants of Kate's apartment complex were several single men who seemed to be besieged by an army of females. They worked for government agencies, sub-agencies, lobbyists and various organizations located in the suburbs. It was very important whom you knew. Name-droppers were everywhere—a culture completely foreign to Kate. She learned that "close friend" didn't mean that at all, and she spent most of her spare time with Special Forces friends and the teachers in the Falls Church school where she was now working full-time.

When summer came there were parties around her apartment house pool and one Saturday she found herself talking with an older man who reminded her of Peter Gulden— smooth, an onlooker. "Happy bunch out here," he said, looking around. "I hope they can swim," as a blonde was pushed into the pool holding her drink.

The blonde came up with the glass still in her hand, and Kate laughed, "Not to worry." The man's name was Alex and he had come to Washington from Montana. She added, "I'm from Wyoming so we're both from the Wild West. Isn't anyone born in the District of Columbia?"

After that they saw each other occasionally and went out for dinner a couple of times, but when school started, Alex was away on a business trip and Kate had little time for socializing. One evening in early November he dropped in. They had just settled down with drinks and a bowl of popcorn when the doorbell rang. It was Ivan. "Am I interrupting something?" He backed away, looking mischievous.

"No, no. Come on in. I want you two to meet. Alex, this is Bob Herrick, my friend from Green Beret times in Germany. Ivan, Alex Paderewski."

"I'll bet you play the frigging piano!" Ivan
added some words in Polish that sounded like a
challenge to mortal combat. Kate decided he'd
been drinking and prepared herself for the worst.
    "No, I don't play the piano." Alex was curt,
not laughing. "Nice to meet you," he said cold-
ly. "I was just going."
    "Please stay." Ivan was ultra-polite, baiting
him. "We can get to know each other."
    "Thank you for the drink, Kate." Alex went
out the door with some difficulty because Ivan
was blocking his exit.
    Kate held her head with both hands, groan-
ing. "Just like old times—joking with total
strangers!"
    "But fun, isn't it, dear one? Most of 'em
don't know what the hell we're talking about.
No sense of humor."
    "You ought to be ashamed! So rude! Weird!"
    "Oh, come off it! Why? Every `leg' needs
shaking up now and then. Gives 'em religion!"
He remembered his limp and the fact he was a
`leg' himself now and his eyes went dull.
    Kate saw the change, guessing its cause, and
clapped him on the back. "Right! Give 'em
hell!" She brought him a beer and they finished
the popcorn.
    "I heard today from one of the fellows that
Ed Kish is back from Vietnam, in the hospital
with some kind of a war injury," Ivan said. "I
don't think they know what it is."
    "Let's go visit him," Kate suggested. "Ed is
a really nice guy. Where is Cassie? Is she with
him?"
    "Here in town, I think," answered Ivan. "I
can find out." They were both silent. Kate took
the popcorn bowls to the kitchen and returned to
find Ivan examining her small icon souvenir
from Mistra.
    "Do you think we could make a go of it?"
Ivan asked suddenly.
    She decided he wasn't drunk and answered

slowly, "You did ask me to marry you once if that's what you mean."

"That's what I mean exactly and I remember you refused. Could you change your mind now that I've got a bum leg and we're both alone? We could rescue each other. Oh hell, this sounds like a speech and what I mean is—I guess I've been in love with you a long time. Come here."

"You guess?" She sat on the sofa beside him. He put an arm around her and they kissed tentatively, a long, but not very satisfactory kiss—their first that was different from friendly pecks on the cheek.

She pulled away. "Give it up. This is way out of character. I'm lost, Ivan. I don't know if you can rescue me, and I don't know if I can rescue you."

"Not too promising but better than the last time I asked. We're not getting any damn younger, Babe."

"You said that once before, —about me." Ivan tried to remember when.

Time stretched into a succession of days and nights, and Kate's new relationship with Ivan became less strange to both of them. Sometimes a week went by and Kate didn't hear from him—telling herself not to care one way or the other. 'Would I really want him to be somebody he isn't? Housebroken? Less of a fighter? Predictable, God forbid?'

Ivan himself was having second thoughts. 'This shit leg! She probably doesn't want to be hooked up with a cripple'—an exaggeration but he was feeling sorry for himself. 'She wants Devorian. Well, he's not here and I am!' He phoned Kate in such a belligerent mood she was worried and asked if he was all right.

"Hell yes! Can I come over or not?"

"Sure. Come on," she answered faintly and put on the coffee pot in case he needed sobering up.

A few minutes later Ivan charged in the door,

his voice loud, "Are you going to marry me or not? Make up your silly mind!" He grabbed her, squeezing until she gasped, "Yes" instead of the `no' she had planned—and stopped struggling.

When Christmas vacation began a Justice of the Peace married them with only Dave and Helen as witnesses. That same evening they flew to Vienna where Ivan had some errand business for the State Department—mixed business and honeymoon, he called it.

In the Vienna airport Ivan picked up their bags and hailed a cab. The darkness of a winter morning lightened as they rode into the city. By the time they reached their hotel in the old part of town, shops were opening and a few people were walking briskly in the streets, their breath turning white in the cold air.

The hotel room was warm, and Federkissen piled on the bed looked inviting. Room service brought coffee and croissants. Kate shivered as she sipped steaming coffee and nibbled on a croissant. They avoided each other's eyes. Ivan pulled the heavy drapes to shut out some of the light...`Is she thinking about Devorian?'

Actually she was thinking, `This is like marrying a brother!' She said from under the bed covers, "You need a shave. Your face is bristly!"

"Is zat so!" He joined her, dropping his clothes on the floor. Their lovemaking was fierce, demanding, and it sent the world a safe distance away. After awhile Ivan whispered, "You were wonderful, baby!" but she was already asleep. He stroked her tangle of red hair, remembered to change the clock to local time, set the alarm for the middle of the afternoon and fell into a deep sleep.

When the alarm went off, Ivan told her he had to see a couple of guys. He'd be back in two hours. He kissed her and she yawned, mumbling, "Okay", before going to sleep again. He hung a DO NOT DISTURB sign on the door and went down the elevator and into the hotel lobby, whistling. Suddenly he struck his head with the flat of his hand. He'd forgotten his morning drink. No matter. He felt fine.

Part of the next week Kate was alone and found herself fighting a private battle, exorcising demons. Window shopping in Kaerntnerstrasse, she saw an elegant bridal gown sewn with seed pearls and remembered her dress borrowed from Helen, so simple but so much more beautiful than the one in the window; and she splurged on Kaffee mit Schlagober at Demel's which did not taste as good as the Bier in Reutberg Gasthof when Jim was beside her. She roamed around back streets in the center of the old city for hours, but it was only a brief escape from reality.

Ivan had one afternoon free and they went into St. Stephan's Cathedral. The organ was playing and the sound rolled and moved around them grandly, subsiding and swelling—heart thumping. They stood still in a side chapel listening, holding hands, and closer than they had ever been. As they stepped outside into the gray early evening light, it was snowing huge flakes, tickling their faces, and Ivan said, "We ought to live in Europe. There's something about being here. Great music! We'll get around, travel on my business account, not stuck in one little boring place in the suburbs—any suburbs."

That night they had dinner at the Griechenbeisel, one of Vienna's oldest inns near the Danube Canal. A light snow was still falling and Washington seemed far away as they went in, bending their heads under low doorways and ceilings. The walls of the tiny room where Herr Ober seated them were dark with generations of smoke. A lantern on their table cast a warm candle glow and somewhere a violin was playing "Wien, Wien, nur du allein—" Kate was flushed, happy. "This is a lot better than teaching school!"

"It damn well better be! It's costing us a fortune!"

"Don't worry. I'll wash dishes if we run out of traveler's checks." Across the small table they looked into each other's eyes, smiling. She had had a way of listening, giving her full attention, that had changed since Devorian's death, as if his ghost were between them. Now in the halo of candlelight she was her old self, there with him, listening with her gray eyes alive, hearing him. They would be all right, he thought, relaxing in the pleasure of the evening and the warm smoothness of wine. The violinist was beginning a gypsy melody in a minor key.

"I need you, Kate, and damn it, you need me!"

"Yes, Ivan. We'll be good for each other." She touched his hand and the solace was more powerful because of its underlying sadness and the strong wine. Herr Ober thought they were a very handsome and happy couple.

"Wouldn't it be wonderful if we could live in Europe?" she asked wistfully.

"But we'd miss football! On the other hand, soccer is a pure art form—and the music! Wow! What music! Anyway, Babe, my job takes us around the globe so we can have it both ways. All you have to do is quit teaching ankle biters and we can live it up!"

"Why not!" she agreed with enthusiasm, "The best of two worlds!"

If her voice sounded a little hollow thinking of how it might have been, Ivan didn't notice. He ordered more Hungarian wine. "Tomorrow let's hear the Wiener Knabenchor, and how about the Lippizaner horses before we leave?"

"Have you got time?" Kate asked.

"I'll make time. This is our honeymoon, Babe!"

Their waiter appeared with the first course, a steaming tureen of soup. He placed it on a serving table and ladled generous portions into their soup plates. The perfume of shredded beef, and vegetables seasoned with paprika, garlic and parsley, was so inviting, Kate took a quick sip. "Careful. It's hot," she warned.

Ivan put down his soupspoon. His eyes followed a girl being seated at a nearby table with her escort, a tall, thin, balding man with cavernous dark eyes and high cheek bones—a Slavic face. Kate felt a healthy twinge of jealousy. The woman was a lot younger than her escort and quite beautiful in an intense sort of way, even with the ragged scar across one cheek. Her hair was long and black with wings of white swept back over her ears; she wore silver hoop earrings and a black dress stunning in its simplicity.

"Do you know them?" Kate asked.

Ivan nodded at the man who returned the nod. "Yes, he's head of the Hungarian Trade Commission attending our conference here— brilliant guy but hard to deal with. And the dame with him—name is Vera, if I remember correctly. I'm surprised she's in Vienna." Ivan looked thoughtful. "I'll tell you later." The woman glanced at Ivan with a puzzled expression as if trying to decide who he was. But then, most women were aware of Ivan.

Snow was drifting silently higher when Ivan called a cab. Kate sat close to him. "Does this remind you of anything?"

"Yeah, the sleigh ride you talked me into." Neither of them mentioned skiing although he was remembering that too. It was unlikely he would be making designs in fresh snow on a steep mountainside again. They were quiet all the way to the hotel hearing the slish of tires and slide of snowflakes against the taxi windows. Too many subjects were taboo between them.

"Good I brought my high boots," she said as they went in. While he picked up the key she decided not to question him about the woman; however, later in spite of herself, she asked, "Who was the woman with the scar? Is she

Hungarian?"

"Yes", answered Ivan, "probably just a little cog in a big machine."

"Sounds like a melodrama," Kate sighed. "Aren't you going to tell me who she is?"

"Tomorrow." Ivan was smug—and tired after a long day and too many glasses of wine. Somehow Vienna no longer seemed as promising as before.

The next day Kate heard the Vienna Boys' Choir alone because Ivan phoned her at noon saying it was impossible to get out of the afternoon meeting. "Gotta earn my keep," he ended glumly.

She waited until that night when they were in the middle of a heavy supper of Schweinhaxe in the Rathaus Keller. "Are you going to tell me about the beautiful Vera or not? Is she a Commie spy or something? And what do you have to do with it? Or am I not supposed to know?"

"Oh it's not like that at all," he assured her. "Years ago her grandfather was a part-time CIA double agent type in Hungary. It was during the Hungarian Uprising in '56. He probably turned in quite a few of his countrymen to the police. Never managed to do us any harm, and all that's water under the bridge. Before it was over he was killed. Nobody was sure which side did it. Vera may have learned something at her grandfather's knee—a long time ago."

Ivan ate some meat and broke off a piece of Brotchen to dip in the juice. Kate sipped her beer, watching him. Ivan continued, "As to how I know her—I saw a photo of her in a briefing once. That's a face you don't forget—not good for engaging in nefarious schemes!" He ruffled Kate's hair and slid his hand down the nape of her neck to her shoulders. "Don't ever try espionage, Babe. Your shade of red hair's too easy to remember." If he didn't intend to pursue the subject of Vera, that was fine with Kate. It was one of their good days.

CHAPTER TWENTY-TWO

They were supposed to leave Vienna on Saturday, but at the last minute Ivan told her he had to stay on. She'd have to go home alone and he'd follow as soon as he could. The conference was nearing a breakthrough, and he was needed because he knew the key people as well as their various languages.

After Ivan left her at the airport and just before she boarded her plane, she wasn't really very surprised to see the face of the dark Hungarian trade official, Vera's escort, staring at her from the front page of a newspaper. The headline was "LEICHE IM DONAU KANAL." Did he drown himself in the Danube or had somebody pushed him? Kate resigned herself to never finding out any more about it. She was sure now—had suspected for a long time—that Ivan was somehow connected with the Agency, along with at least a fourth of the population in Washington. His qualifications were certainly good. Why worry? Anyway, he could take care of himself and he never seemed to mix alcohol with work.

Ivan was two separate people, she thought as the stewardess began her safety pitch, one flippant, one serious. She remembered his description of his background—the son of a Hungarian singer, Aniko, and an American father who played the drums. They had met and married during a cross-country tour with a theatrical company. According to Ivan, his mother had to leave the last performance of Abie's Irish Rose and barely made it to the hospital in Albuquerque where he was born. His father didn't see him 'til the next day because the cast had an all-night party where he found Aniko's replacement in the play unusually attractive. Ivan's childhood was a series of backstage nannies who often turned out to be prop boys.

As he grew up he was in and out of various

jobs until he finally won enough in a poker game to get himself into UCLA majoring in languages. An army recruiter took one look at his academic record and put him on the fast track which wasn't very helpful, he told Kate, because in Korea they weren't digging foxholes deep enough to accommodate his 6 feet 2, especially if other occupants had arrived before him. By this time, he could swear in Chinese with a Korean accent. Kate gave up trying to stay awake, tucked a pillow behind her head and the rest of the flight was a blur.

Days later she was driving Ivan home from the airport. "You have multiple choice," she quipped. "(a) Yes (b) No (c) Part-time. The question is: Do you work for the Agency?"

"(c)," he answered. "Any more questions?"

"When I happen to be on vacation, can I tag along?"

"Sure, kid! My occasional role is minor, not very exciting. In fact, 99% of my travels are quite legit, so when you're not in school, like the saying goes, we'll see the world!"

He changed the subject. "The first thing we're going to do, Babe, is move out of your condo and my so-called apartment. We need space to turn around, not two chicken coops!"

"Great! When do we start looking?" At the prospect of a new home, Kate almost missed her turn off the Beltway. Then she remembered to ask, "By the way, is it your place or mine tonight?"

"Yours, Babe. There's nothing in my fridge except beer.

Tomorrow would be as good a time as any to begin looking for a house." He caught Kate's sideways glance and added, "Why don't you ask Helen to help since I'll be working out of town for a few days? Catch up with you when I get back."

"Okay. I'll estimate your bankroll!" Kate giggled.

"Well, just be sure you wait 'til I get back to sign on the dotted line." Ivan groaned loudly. "I have to play the races first."

A week later Kate found a newly built house in Falls Church. It needed only a few changes, a bigger bay window in the kitchen next to the deck and some built-in bookcases by the fireplace, to meet their requirements. In two weeks the paperwork was done and they closed, owners of their first home.

The following weekend, Kate intended to spend some time in the new place deciding where their odds and ends of furnishings would fit. She found it hard to concentrate. The empty walls were a challenge, asking, silent voices in her ear, "How are you going to make us into a real home? How can you keep up the pretense?"

She held her hands over her ears as if that would stop the voices. Ivan was coming back that night. Better to postpone this chore until later.

With the move, his work, her teaching, and the coming and going of friends stationed at the Pentagon, their days were filled. Finally, one morning when cherry blossoms were in bloom and white fleecy clouds floated above the Potomac, the urge to travel grew in Kate like roots below the ground, reaching for the sun. "Why am I moldering away in school," Kate said to herself, "when I could be in all sorts of interesting places?"

Ivan returned that night from another trade conference, and on the way home from the airport, she asked him if they needed her teaching salary to keep up with the Joneses.

"Hell no!" he exclaimed. "I thought you were enjoying it. Quit tomorrow if you want to."

"I don't want to just sit at home," she countered. "I want to go off to faraway places—if you want to drag me along." She ended on a questioning note.

"Listen, ninny, of course I want you along.

But it might not be as much fun as you think.
You'd be on your own a lot while I'm off doing
my errands."
       "I'm a big girl. I'd manage. After all, I've
driven a car through Paris, Athens, Rome, —"
       "Proof of the pudding, Babe. Let's do it!"
       So in June Kate resigned her job and their
lives changed. She wondered if their tomorrows
would turn out better, or not as exciting as she
had imagined.
       In the late '70s an Air Force friend from
early years in Bad Tölz and his wife were in
town. Dave and Helen invited the two couples
for dinner. Conversation went back to the time
of the Air Force Survival School when Kate had
their daughter in third grade, recalling vintage
stories about people they remembered. Kate had
heard the tale of the naked escapee a dozen
times. When the major began to tell it, she wondered what new flourishes would be in this version.
       "You were there, may not have heard this
story," he gestured with his fork, "but Marge
wasn't, so help me out if I miss something. The
Survival School lasted only a year as comple-
ment to the 10th, when a news magazine highlighted some of their training methods and upset
mothers got through to their congressmen."
       Everyone tried to look interested. It really
was a good story and mostly true. He continued.
"A general decided to get out of the flak and
close the school before he lost his star.
That was in 1955. It was this way, honey," ignor-
ing his wife's resigned expression. "It was like a
game of survival. If "aggressors" captured students at the school left in the middle of a
Bavarian forest, they were put in prison in the
Kaserne basement and interrogated. If they
escaped and reached the Commanding Officer
by telephone, they were free. One creative fellow declared he was dead and was surprised to
find himself on a cold concrete slab for the

night. Another one escaped and ran naked into
the Post beauty shop, grabbing a towel from a
lady under a hair dryer. He reached the phone
just as his pursuers rushed in. They carried him
out kicking and hollering, leaving a row of
astonished ladies in curlers, with their eyes popping out." The major's audience laughed appre-
ciatively.

Inevitably, after dessert, the visiting major
asked, "Where's Jim Devorian these days? Ivan,
you were his buddy, you and Hunk."

Ivan took the plunge. "He was with me in
Nam, killed in the Battle of To Canh."

"I'm sorry to hear that! I hadn't heard, but I
don't see the old 10th SFs since I left Tölz. It
was a nasty war. I was further south—Sky
raiders."

Helen called Kate to help load the dishwash-
er, and the other woman joined them saying,
"Let them talk old times. They never get tired of
it!" Helen could see that Kate was shaken and
changed the subject to the price of endive in the
commissary, banging dishes to cover something,
she wasn't sure what. At least it would take
attention away from Kate's face.

Sometimes Kate found herself wondering
why Ivan had survived and Jim was dead. Times
like the have-to-go-to function in Georgetown,
when Ivan was standing by the buffet table and
spotted her across the room talking to a very
important congressman from California. One of
those unexplainable silences developed just as
he called to her, grinning, "Babe ol'girl, you better get over here. I opine these are fresh, not
frozen shrimp."

The evening was dull, and Kate felt like
playing the game. Maybe it was the champagne.
She gave Ivan a wicked look. "Put some in your
pocket for me," she called back in a stage whisper. A ripple of laughter went through the room,
the sharp edge gone from the party.

But when the hostess lifted one penciled

eyebrow, the room was still again. She smiled icily, "I'm so glad we have the seal of approval!"

On the way home Ivan grinned, "We have a hell of a lot of fun at stuffy parties, don't we, Babe!"

"Like old times," she murmured in his ear. "We've just been crossed off another guest list."

He looked at her approvingly out of the corner of his eye as he drove into their garage. "You're so ga-awgeous!"

"Oh, Rhett," she purred. "Y'all must carry me into our mansion."

He got out of the car and with a mighty effort, hoisted her over his shoulder like a sack of wheat. He stumbled toward the door, fumbling for the key with one hand. "You're getting a lot heavier than you used to be," he grunted.

Moments went by and then he heard a chuckle somewhere behind his left ear. "Frankly, my dear—," Kate giggled, "I don't give a damn!"

They awoke the next morning with hangovers. Ivan left after an urgent call from the office and Kate dragged herself to the kitchen where she drank two cups of strong coffee. She had time to reflect. He always pulls these stunts in high society situations. He's obnoxious just to show everybody else is an ass. Actually, they were! The lady archbishop was so proper, looking down her long nose. Kate laughed but it turned into a hiccup. She took an aspirin, rubbed her eyes and crawled back in bed.

Much later, thinking about the incident of the fresh shrimp, Kate believed the party was the downward turning point in their marriage—such a little thing, childish, but extraordinarily potent for its minuscule importance at the time.

At noon the phone rang, awakening her. Ivan said, "I won't be home until around six. We're flying to Munich tomorrow. Go shopping and buy yourself some clothes. Sky's the limit." Kate was mollified but wary. Would they be going to Bad Tölz? Memories dredged up? She did not have time to ask questions. He had already hung up.

Kate lay still in bed, pondering. Not a good idea to go to Munich. Suppose Ivan wanted to go to Tölz, his old stamping ground, or Garmisch. What excuse could she make? He'd know she was remembering Jim, and she couldn't hide it.

A bright beam of sunshine glinted on a glass bird feeder outside the bedroom window. Kate blinked; her stomach still felt queasy. I haven't made Ivan very happy though we've had our moments—.

She pushed back the covers, picked up the phone, and dialed his office. "Ivan," her voice matter-of-fact, "I've got a dentist's appointment in two days and if he doesn't finish pasting a crown on my front tooth, it's going to fall out while we're on the trip. Not only that, but Friday I have to help Helen run a rummage sale for her hospital charity. Can I take a raincheck?"

"Well, if you can't make it. Maybe you could fly over next week if I'm still there. I was counting on having you with me, Babe. We could see if our favorite places are still there."

Kate felt a twinge of guilt. "You know Munich's the city I love most in the whole world. If you're in Munich next week, I'll come over. Remember the time we were thrown out of the Regina Hotel bar?" He laughed, and she almost changed her mind.

CHAPTER TWENTY-THREE

After Ivan left, Kate was at loose ends. She
longed to tell Jim what was happening in her
life. When she opened the connecting door to the
garage, she intended to make her weekly pil-
grimage to Jim's grave. But once behind the
wheel, Kate put the key in the ignition and sat
still, unable to remember her destination. She
started for the mall, thinking it would come back
to her.

At the corner of the block where she always
turned on her way to Arlington, she suddenly
knew where she was going. "Am I crazy?" she
groaned and whipped the car into a U-turn, nearly knocking over a tricycle left by the curb. "I
need a shrink!" she exclaimed panic-stricken,
and back in her own driveway, slammed on the
brakes. She caught a glimpse of her own distort-
ed face in the rearview mirror, as if the mirror
were cracked.

A neighbor, who was mowing his lawn,
came over. "Need some help?" he offered.

Kate shook her head, unable to speak, and
hurried into the house. The garage doors came
down.

Inside, she frowned. I must be losing my
mind! The shadows in the hallway reminded her
of the dark hall in her Bad Tölz quarters that terrible day when the chaplain knocked at her door.
She shivered. I need someone to talk to, but
whom? Don't feel like putting on a cheerful face
for Helen. In fact, she hasn't been very receptive
lately—rather shop than talk like we used to.

Cassie and Ed Kish flashed into her mind.
She had neglected her old friends and it was
time to look them up. Kate called the number
listed under Edward Kish in the phonebook and
recognized Cassie's voice. Kate answered,
"Hello, Cass," and Cassie knew immediately
who it was.

"Oh Kate, it's wonderful to hear from you!

Where are you?" Kate gave her the address and
telephone number, waiting for her to write it
down. Cassie sounded giddy, almost crying. "Oh
Kate darling, you don't know how happy I am to
talk to you. Ed is going through treatment at
Walter Reed. He has some kind of rare disease
he may have picked up in Nam and he's very
sick. I feel so alone. It's a miracle you're here
and called. Oh, I want to see you! Can you possibly come over and spend the afternoon with
me Thursday? The doctors will be giving Ed a
lot of strenuous tests and want him to stay there
and rest overnight, so I'll be home."

She stopped for breath, and Kate broke in,
"Of course I'll come, Cassie. Yes, Thursday will
be fine. Now tell me where you live. We'll save
all the news 'til I see you." Kate hung up, wondering why she was always around when Cassie
was in trouble. Shaking her head, she made up
her mind. It won't hurt me to be a port in another storm. Poor Ed. I hope he isn't as ill as it
sounds.

Thursday, Kate followed her pencil map to
Cassie's townhouse in a large housing complex
across town. She resolved not to mention her
own problems. Cassie had enough to worry
about. She rang the doorbell and the door
opened before the chimes stopped ringing.
Cassie had evidently been watching for her from
the window. She threw her arms around Kate.
Finally the two women held each other apart and
took stock. Kate's voice was warm. "You look
young, Cassie! I thought you'd be an old crone
like me."

"My wrinkles aren't showing—just because
you're here, dearest Kate! You don't look any
older than the last time I saw you in Bad Tölz a
million years ago. Same shiny red on top." She
touched Kate's hair. "Are you sure you don't dye
it? Well, maybe I see a few gray hairs here and
there—and still as slim as ever."

"Not true, Cass. You look mighty good to

me. Life with Ed has kept you young. Tell me, what's wrong with his health?"

Cassie's face clouded. "Come on out in the kitchen and we'll have a cup of coffee and some Texas sheet cake I made last night. I'll tell you what I know, which isn't much."

Kate looked around the spic and span kitchen with red-checked curtains at the windows. Cassie's Bavarian blue and gray salt-glaze crocks and jars were in neat rows, used for flour, sugar, and salt. Others decorated a hanging shelf over the stove. Kate sat down at the breakfast table while Cassie bustled around making coffee and cutting the cake. She waited.

"I'm so worried about Ed." Cassie's voice broke. "The doctors don't seem to know what's the matter. They have him fill out stacks of questionnaires—about Vietnam, whether he ever took drugs, ate monkey meat with the Montagnards, was injured by a pungi stake, where he worked in Michigan, what his parents died of—I can't tell you all the stuff. He's had so many blood tests, it's no wonder he feels weak as a baby."

Kate drank a quick sip of coffee. "I can't picture Ed weak as a baby. What's the prognosis? How long until he's back to normal?"

"The doctors won't say one way or another. That's what's driving me crazy." Cassie twisted and re-twisted a lock of mousy hair hanging in front of her ear. Kate decided it was a gesture only slightly more tolerable than her old habit of tweaking her nose from side to side.

Cassie burst out, "Why did this happen to Ed? He's the dearest, most gentle man I ever met. He won't even kill a spider since he came back from Nam, says the best duty he had in Nam was helping mountain people grow food crops and protect their villages. But violence and killing. He saw too much of it. Now this sickness. The generals are all healthy, you can bet." She was twisting the lock of hair until it stood out stiffly from her head.

"I'm so sorry, Cass." Kate set down her cup and squeezed Cassie's hand to keep it away from her hair. "Just don't let Ed see how upset you are. The more optimistic he feels, the sooner he'll get better. You have to believe it. Right now Ivan's in Munich on business. When he's back, we'll visit Ed in the hospital or here if he's home. Ivan will want to see for himself how he's doing. Ed was on his team and one of his favorites in the whole 10th. They'll have lots to talk about."

"That would really please Ed. I'll tell him he has a surprise coming." Cassie's face glowed.

"This wonderful cake is going to ruin my girlish figure. But I don't care." Kate smiled at her friend and took another bite. "I do a lot of walking with Helen around the malls—you remember Helen, and—." She stopped on the brink of telling about her visits to Arlington Cemetery.

Suddenly Cassie broke through the wall of silence between them. "Oh Kate, I feel so guilty! I've never told Ed about that time—you know, when I—-had to have—" she sobbed, "an— abortion. It's haunted me all these years, night and day. How can I tell him? He'll never trust me—-again!"

Kate put her arms around Cassie, gave her a handkerchief, and held her tight.

"Sorry, Kate," Cassie sniffled, wiping her eyes. "But you're the only one in the world I can talk to."

Kate patted her shoulder. "Cassie, if you tell him this story out of the dim and distant past, you will probably feel relieved for about five seconds or less. Then you'll see how upset he is. Why hurt him? For what? My advice is, forget the whole thing. Take it or leave it. That's for you to decide."

Cassie nodded slowly. "You always see things so clearly. You're right. I have to think of

Ed. I do love him so much."

Kate's throat was parched. She poured herself a glass of water, added ice and drank it thirstily while Cassie leaned on the table with her head in her hands. Now it was Kate's turn. She hesitated and then blurted out, "I envy you, Cass."

Cassie lifted her head and stared at her in amazement. "Why, Kate? Surely you've been married to two wonderful men. Oh, I know you lost Major Devorian so soon and, of course, that was a terrible shock, but now you are the wife of Colonel Herrick." Something in Kate's face made her uncertain, but she blundered on. "He's so handsome and so smart and you must live in a beautiful home, have lots of important friends, and——."

Kate interrupted, "But Cass." She stopped. Cassie looked at her, wide-eyed. It came out in a rush. "I go to Arlington Cemetery almost every week to be with Jim. Ivan doesn't know it. So you see, we both have secrets. And mine isn't in the dim and distant past."

It was Cassie's turn to be the mother, but she couldn't think of any way to comfort, much less counsel, Kate. "I'm so inadequate," she moaned. "If only I could help, after all you've done for me. I'm so sorry!"

Outside the window a cat was chasing a squirrel. The squirrel ran up a tree, flirting its tail, teasing the cat. Kate thought, I've been chasing things I've never caught all my life. She was bone-weary. "That's OK," she said. "It's good to have somebody I can trust. Sorry to burden you when you are so worried about Ed."

But Cassie almost beamed. "Finally I can do something after all these years—just a little something for you!"

"Time to go, Cass. Thanks, my dear, for the cake and coffee and for listening. Let's get together again soon at my house. Call me when you have news about Ed and give him my love."

Cassie, her pudgy face anxious, stood on the
doorstep gazing after Kate's car until it was out
of sight.

Kate drove into her garage, totally disgusted
with herself. I've blown my damn cover, spilled
my guts. She raced into the house and let the
warm jacket, which was choking her fall on the
floor. A New Yorker magazine on the table
caught her eye. Just the brittle, know-it-all stuff
to blast me out of this lowdown mood. She
picked up the magazine and turned its pages, but
the words blurred.

CHAPTER TWENTY-FOUR

Ivan's business in Munich lasted only four days so his plan for Kate to join him fell through, and he came home tired and out-of-sorts. "The next time I'm sent out, Babe, you're going with me! I don't care if it's Podunk! Even if your teeth are falling out!"

"I'll drop everything including teeth and go," she promised, resolving to put her heart into the next journey, no matter if the destination turned out to be the North Pole. She made a face. "Are you ever posted to Spitzbergen?"

"No, but maybe Nebraska."

"Let's make a bargain. It has to be overseas."

"You got it." He stuck his head in the newspaper, leaving her to unpack his bags.

Later over dinner she asked, "Aren't you going to tell me about my favorite city?"

"Oh yeah. Well I wasn't there long enough to do much looking around, but I can tell you, the traffic is something else! From Marienplatz down to the station is jammed with Beatle imitations—jugglers, fruit peddlers, you name it. Remember when more bicycles than VWs were wheeling down that street?"

She nodded. "You had just arrived. Early Fifties."

"I walked down there the second morning," Ivan went on, "and—let's see—I heard Figaro at the Cuvilliés one night—not as good as when I heard it with Hermann Prey. That's all the playing around I had time for. The rest was business. Didn't even get a beer in the Hofbrauhaus. And I missed a new exhibit at the Alte Pinokotek."

"How was the weather?" she asked, refilling his glass of wine.

"Not great. Typical dark November. Cloudy with rain part of the time. Too early for the Christkindlmarkt, or I would have brought you a bauble."

"An emerald?" Kate teased.

"They only sell glass ones at the
Christkindlmarkt. I'd have to go to Eichmann's
for the real thing."

Kate piled their dishes and went to the
kitchen where she busied herself scooping butter
pecan ice cream into bowls. Jim's diamond was
warm under her shirt. She brought the bowls and
a plate of cookies to the table. Her voice was
even. "You remember Ed Kish. We were going
to look up Ed and Cassie before your trip to
Munich. Well, I went to see Cassie while you
were gone. Ed is in and out of the hospital. He
has some kind of disease—the doctors can't
seem to find out what it is—maybe from Nam. I
told her you'd want to see him when you came
home. You do want to see him don't you?"

"Damn right I do!" Ivan put down his spoon
with a heavy sigh. "Find out where he is, and I'll
try to get off early tomorrow and pick you up on
the way."

Kate went to the phone and called Cassie.
She came back to the table. "Ed is in Walter
Reed again. She'll meet us at the main visitors'
entrance. I said I'd call her back when you know
what time you can make it."

"Why the hell can't they find out what's the
matter?" Ivan frowned across the table at Kate.
There was no need to answer. He gulped down
the rest of the wine in his glass.

That night Kate went to bed early. She could
hear Ivan moving around the den, changing TV
channels—the rustle of papers. In the kitchen
the refrigerator door slammed. He dropped
something heavy, probably a book. Kate heard a
loud exclamation, "Crap!" followed by the
sound of a cork popping, and a gurgle as he
poured himself a drink. She pulled the covers
over her head.

The next morning Ivan was glum and in a
hurry. He swallowed two cups of coffee,
grabbed his briefcase, and left for the office. She
called after him, "Don't forget to let me know

when you're coming home."

She wasn't sure he heard, but at midday he phoned. "I can be home by 2:30. Tell Cassie we'll meet her at about 3:15. Okay with you?"

"Fine. I'll get some fruit to take him."

Cassie was waiting for them just inside the main door of the hospital. "It's so nice of you to come. Ed will be so happy to see you. I haven't told him you're coming."

Ivan bent down and gave her a brief hug. "Good to see you again, Cassie. Where is he?" She gestured toward a long hallway. A light flashed the arrival of an elevator. It disgorged a load of passengers and the medicinal smell of disinfectants. Ivan and Kate followed Cassie in and held the elevator open for a white-coated attendant pushing an amputee in a wheelchair. Ivan broke the silence. "How's Ed doing? What does his doctor say?"

"That's the trouble." Cassie sighed and fished in her purse for a handkerchief. "They don't say. Ed's getting discouraged, but he tries to hide it from me. We're both pretending as hard as we can." She sniffed and wiped her nose.

The elevator stopped at their floor and they walked down a corridor, branching off to the right. Around the corner three empty wheelchairs stood against the wall. A nurse passed them with a trolley of medicines. Ivan tried to prevent the onslaught of Cassie's tears with his most cheerful tone. "He'll be fine, Cassie. Ed's too tough to let whatever it is get him down."

Cassie knocked on a half-open door and Ivan and Kate followed her in. What they saw was a shock. Kate felt Ivan stiffen, but he walked firmly to the bed, grinning down at his old friend. "You old bastard! What are you trying to do, ol' buddy, lay a bunch of nurses? I saw some lookers on the way up here!"

Ed's ashen face brightened with surprise and he tried to wink. "Don't tell on me," he rasped. His hand reaching for Ivan's flopped down on the sheet and Ivan put both of his hands around it with a gentle squeeze.

"We brought you some fruit," Kate smiled. She makes a place for the basket between a plastic pitcher and a box of Kleenex on the narrow table over his bed, and gave him a kiss.

"I told her you'd rather have a pint of whiskey, but she wouldn't listen. I'll sneak one in another day ol' pal—better medicine than you'll get in this joint!"

Ivan was overdoing the jocular bit, Kate decided. Better leave them alone for a few minutes. She was sure Ivan could carry on a conversation single-handed. She beckoned Cassie, saying, "This room is too little for four of us. You guys talk about old times and we'll be back shortly."

Before they closed the door behind them, Kate saw Ivan draw a chair close to the bed and heard him say, "I've been thinking about that time we were in Visegrad. Do you remember—"

Cassie and Kate walked down the corridor past several potted palms that looked as if they had not been watered lately and found a small sitting area no bigger than an alcove. Cassie was shaking. "What am I going to do if something happens to Ed? My sister's in California and since we moved here from Detroit, I don't know many people—except you. You're always around when I need you—just like an angel!"

There were four folding chairs around a small wooden table with some old dilapidated magazines and a bible on top. They pulled two chairs out and sat down. Kate tried to change the subject. "Remember Angel? She dumped Hunk as soon as they were married, or did I tell you? Nobody hears from her anymore."

"Yes, I remember her. She always got what she wanted. I never did until I met Ed, and I never would have met him if it hadn't been for you."

"That was pure happenstance." Kate's tone was as cheerful as she could muster remembering her own brief moments with Jim. "You've had some great years together. Now try to take it a day at a time. This illness of Ed's may be a passing thing. Anyway, I want you to call on us day or night if you need help. I'll be around even if Ivan's away. You can count on it."

The claustrophobic little room seemed to get smaller. A family with two children crowded in, dropping their toy cars on the floor, and Cassie and Kate went back to Ed's room. His face was flushed, his eyes brighter. He was propped up on his pillows. "Gotta go, ol' buddy," Ivan told him. "I'll be back, maybe even tomorrow if the boss lets me loose. We'll talk Hungarian for ol' time's sake."

"Thanks," Kish murmured. Cassie kissed him, caressing his cheek and adjusting his pillows. Ed's eyes followed them to the door.

Outside, the heat hung—heavy. The air they breathed was gray with dust. Ivan and Kate went with Cassie to her car. He took her key and opened the driver's side. "Hot enough to fry Goddamn eggs on this door!" Abruptly, he asked, "Who are Ed's doctors?" She gave him the names, one an internist and three specialists. "Tell them I'm Ed's long lost brother—it's true, I am—and I'll talk to them, see what they can tell me about Ed's condition, get back to you. Okay?"

Again Cassie was close to tears. "Would you? How can I ever thank you?"

"No problem, kid." He watched her drive away and wiped the sweat out of his eyes. "Just as hot as Nam but not so much gunfire," he muttered without thinking. But then his voice became too loud in order to cover his blunder. Kate's face had turned chalk-white. "Kish looks bad, Babe. Very bad." They were silent on the way home.

During the next few days Ivan made good on

his promise to talk to Ed's doctors, but gained
little more information than Cassie had told
them. It was evident they had no answers. He
enlisted Dave's help and they found more men
in the area who had known Kish on other assignments. They set up a roster so he would have
visitors almost every day. "A hospital's a lonely
place," Ivan told Kate.

As if I didn't know! Kate thought but said
aloud, "I'm glad you guys stick together." Ivan's
concern for Kish was no surprise to Kate.
Outside they were all tough as nails, inside, soft
as mush. For her part, Kate saw Cassie often,
taking Helen with them for lunch to give Cassie
a break from long vigils at the hospital.
Sometimes Kate hated Cassie for being with her
husband while he fought off death. If only she
could have held Jim safe in her arms, she'd have
stayed with him forever! Never left him alone.
How could she leave Ed even for a minute?

After the Christmas holidays Ed's condition
deteriorated rapidly. He was fed intravenously
and some days he survived only because he was
taken to intensive care. Ivan spent hours of his
spare time sitting with him, talking about ski
trips in Bavaria or silent, touching his hand as
gently as a mother. Once, Cassie arrived in her
husband's room to find Ivan nodding off in the
chair by his bed.

In February Ivan was scheduled for a few
days in Rome. Kate decided not to go along. It
would have meant leaving Cassie without her
support. A major snowstorm hit Washington and
Ivan's departure was delayed for hours. At the
airport he resigned himself to a long wait and
settled in the lounge with a glass of scotch and a
paperback with a lurid cover. Traffic stopped in
the city and its environs. Washington became a
silent city except for the wind. Kate tried to call
Cassie, but telephone lines were down. She
could see nothing moving outside her house
except whirling snow driven by gusts of wind

out of the north.

Snowdrifts piled higher and higher on the sidewalks and roads around Cassie's house. She tried valiantly to shovel a path to the garage but her boots filled with snow, her arms ached, and she realized it would be impossible to get out to the street, let alone reach Walter Reed Hospital. There was nothing to do but pace the floor. The wind moaned around corners of buildings and through cracks between window frames—a lonesome howl like a child crying for its mother. And in the hospital Kish stopped breathing.

CHAPTER TWENTY-FIVE

After his return from Rome, Ivan reported in. His boss looked up from a pile of papers on his desk with a toothy smile. "Sit down, Herrick. I've got great news for you."

"Should I salute before or after I hear it?" Ivan asked. Whitehead was an impossible mealy-mouth ass, would knife you in the back if he could get away with it. Ivan's hands on the leather arms of the chair were relaxed, not revealing his tension.

Whitehead grinned, appreciating the humor. He leaned forward, adjusting his hairpiece with a scrawny hand. "Herrick, you're the luckiest man in the Department. No offense. You've earned it. Your salary will be a lot larger than you're getting now—all sorts of perks, big office. You've been chosen to head up a new section. What do you think of that?"

"Sounds interesting." Ivan's voice was even, noncommittal. "Tell me more."

Whitehead rubbed his hands together. "You have the weekend to think it over. Let me know Monday. Here, take a look." The two men bent over the papers on Whitehead's desk.

At the end of the first day of the new job, Ivan came home in a foul mood. "Why the hell did I say yes? It's a Goddamn bureaucracy and I'm not going to put up with that bunch of shit-heads! I could line 'em up and march 'em around like good little boys, but I'll be dammed if I want to bother." Kate thought silence was the better part of valor, but he took it for disagreement. "You think I can't do the job."

Kate took a beef roast out of the oven. "Of course you can do it, and teach 'em to say uncle besides. But if you don't want to, why should you? We don't need the money."

His face showed his surprise. "You're a good kid, Kate! I guess I'll hang in there until the operation is working like it ought to. Shouldn't

take long. Might be fun. I'd hate to be called a
quitter."

Kate congratulated herself silently. He had
been moody ever since Kish's death, and she
hadn't really done anything to alleviate his obvious pain. "You're no quitter", she assured him.
"Never have been, never will be. But any time
you want to stop working, you have my blessing." Privately, she wondered how Ivan would
fill his time, but her own relentless grief left little room in her heart for him. She put dinner on
the table.

Late the next afternoon Kate was watching
an interview with a Pulitzer Prize author on TV.
She had drawn the drapes and turned on one
lamp in the den. Leaning back in her favorite
lounge chair, munching on a bag of chips, her
feet up on a hassock, she suddenly remembered
an open window in her bedroom. The thick carpet muffled her steps as she padded down the
hall. She did not know Ivan was home from
work and squealed when she discovered him
standing in front of a long mirror by the door.

He looked cross. She knew that look. He was
wide-eyed, startled by her sudden appearance,
but it also meant he could use some reassurance.
She stood beside him and their eyes gazed back
at each other from the mirror. "You're getting
some damn gray hairs too." But he sounded
indifferent and was again absorbed in his reflection. Inspecting a strand of gray at his temple, he
gave it a yank as if he would pull it out by the
roots. Involuntarily Kate's hand moved toward
him but could not reach across the void between
them. His back was rigid. She turned away leaving him still standing in front of the mirror, his
face puzzled, forlorn.

The '87 stock market's plunge, a shock for
many Americans, did not alarm Ivan and Kate.
Their home was paid for and his government
salary showed no signs of diminishing. "What
about the Agency? Will there be cutbacks?"

Kate asked.

They were sitting on the deck overlooking their backyard. Evening light slanted low over the house behind them. Shadows lengthened on the lawn and a flock of sparrows settled in the branches of a tall spruce, making nighttime nesting sounds. Ivan took a swallow of Scotch, ruminating. "Not as long as the Cold War lasts, but who knows how long? There are always cracks in a dictatorship, even in the Soviet Union."

"Do you think so, really?"

Kate's curiosity registered in Ivan's mind and he stood up. "It's getting too dark to see out here." He took the newspaper and his drink inside without answering her question.

Kate did not follow him but sat still in her deck chair, thinking. When Ed was in the hospital taking so long to die, she and Ivan had been close enough to talk to each other in the old way. Now their relationship was on the skids again with long dangerous silences between them. She had tried to keep up with Cassie, but when she called, Cassie always seemed to be busy with church activities, finding comfort in volunteer work. They saw each other infrequently. Helen and Dave were planning to move to Sun City, Arizona, and Kate would miss Helen's hearty laugh more than anything.

It was dark and the night air turned cool. The sensor light over the deck came on. Kate shivered and went inside the house, trying not to think how her life might have been.

In early May her promise to accompany Ivan on his next trip to Europe was put to the test. She had agreed to go along on the second of his assignments in Rome, one of her favorite cities in Italy. Now sitting in an outdoor restaurant in the Piazza Navona on this balmy spring night, she only half regretted her decision to come. It had been too many years since she had seen the wonders of Rome and three whole days were ahead to bring back memories.

Ivan leaned back in his chair in a post-bran-
dial mood, bit off the tip of his Cuban cigar and
called the waiter. "A glass of grappa, per
favore."

The waiter's eyebrows shot up in disdain.
"No, Signor, we do not have. Perhaps in
Trastavere."

"My God! Are we in Italy or Peoria?" Ivan
looked menacing.

"Very sorry, Signor." The waiter held a
match to Ivan's cigar with the utmost deference.
He laid the check on the table and took their
empty plates, stacking the dishes; their edges
even, on his arm.

Kate sighed. She had been sitting beside
Ivan, eyes half closed, indulging herself in the
dream, pretending Jim was with her watching
the fountains in the center of the Piazza Navona.
It had been easy. Quicksilver showers of water
exploded like fireworks in the fountains, an
aphrodisiac. It was as if she were floating on the
bubble surface of the fountain, and silver drops
covered her body, clung to her hair.

Now a pungent whiff of acrid smoke from
Ivan's cigar jolted her back to reality. She was
trembling. Ivan reached for her hand. "Not such
a damn bad job I've got. Right, Babe?"

"Oh right," she answered, thinking, If Jim
were here his fingers would be exploring the
hollows of my palm, counting my fingertips one
by one.'

Ivan did not notice her expression and began
talking, pointing at the middle fountain in front
of them, "The Fountain of the Rivers is really
one of Bernini's masterpieces—hard to believe
it was created around three hundred years ago.
Of course, it's pure Renaissance, couldn't be
mistaken for anything else. This whole piazza
was Domitian's Stadium in Papal Rome." He
interrupted himself. "Oh hell. I sound just like a
guidebook."

"Yes, you do." Kate laughed to assure him she was listening. "But go on. Maybe I'll remember it this time. All those facts just sort of swim around in my head and mix together like a goulash."

Ivan gave her a long calculating look. Was she serious or leading him on? "What are you going to do tomorrow?"

"Oh, fool around, revisit some favorite places. Top of the list is Capitoline Hill." But Ivan was paying the check and did not hear her. She waited until he stubbed out his cigar and then added, "Do you have any time tomorrow when you could sightsee with me?"

"'Fraid not, doll. I'm in prison the whole day and the next—maybe a couple of hours before our flight. We'll find a place to eat in Trastevere tomorrow—better food than in this tourist trap. Anyway, I can get a damn grappa if I want it." He stood up, tossed a few lire to some ragged urchins lurking near their table and hailed a horse-drawn carriage.

Kate felt a pang. He really is a romantic at heart, and I'm having all the fun while he gets no time off. On an impulse she said aloud, "If you ever want to look for my ghost, I'll be sitting in Campodoglia Piazza under the statue of Marcus Aurelius, or maybe on the horse, looking down on the Piazza Venezia."

His face wrinkled in disbelief. "Love of my life, I'll shuffle off this mortal coil long before you do. Let me think. Where in hell will you find my ghost? Not here. More likely in Dante's Inferno."

She laughed and squeezed his hand. It was true. Of all the countries she had known, the very air of Italy, even more than France, was most filled with erotic intimations. Maybe it was the daily saturation of golden light that invited sexual thoughts.

Their driver glanced over his shoulder and decided they were certainly not lovers or by this

time they would be kissing—and not having an
affair, like a lot of American oldies that come to
Rome looking for a gigolo. Probably been married for awhile. He thought of his mistress in
Trastevere. After he delivered these two he'd
drop over to her flat, and she'd better be there.
Basta!

As the world turned, newspaper headlines
became startling. Gorbachev's visit to
Washington greeted by popular acclaim was
amazing enough, but Yeltsin's sudden takeover
left the world gasping and the Agency in disar-
ray. Ivan was away much of the time, going to
meetings, working late. One night he came
home at midnight in a fury and announced, "I'm
putting in my resignation! The smartest fellows
in my section have been transferred. Leaves the
rest of us naked, just when our errands are getting more important!"

Caught by surprise, Kate showed her dismay. "What will you do all day?"

"Go out with the boys. Wanna go along? I
guess not," he added without waiting for an
answer.

"As it happens, I'll be going to my book
club. I suppose that sounds pretty tame to you."

"Well I'd a damn sight rather go to the gym
than the Ladies' Sewing Circle! I know some
young guys still in the military, at the health center. Think I'll go for that in my spare time."

"Can you handle the competition?" As soon
as she said it, Kate regretted her question—too
late—a low blow when he was already miserable.

"Are you kidding? Damn right I can! You
think I can't?"

Kate was on the verge of tears. Not daring to
speak, she only shook her head.

The first day after Ivan quit work, he left the
house, banging the door behind him. "I'll show
her!" he growled and headed for the gym. Later
Kate found him leaning on the front door, bare-

ly able to make it inside the entrance. He was breathing heavily and pale. When she took his arm to help him in he shook her off, muttering, "Leave me alone! I'm no damn baby!" He slumped into the nearest chair and gradually his color returned. "Bring me a drink."

"How about some coffee? I just made a fresh pot." Seeing him scowl, she added, "I'll spike it for you."

"Don't be stingy with the bottle." He was too tired to argue, and when she came back he was snoring, his head tilted down on his chest. She emptied the cup and sat down, almost as weary as he was. She had just returned from a visit to Jim's grave. Often on these occasions she heard the gun salute and Taps from one of the many graveside services that took place every day in the cemetery. Seeing the young widows, some in their early twenties, haunted her until she began to have nightmares about flying over Jim's open grave.

Now Kate sat listening to Ivan's deep breathing. She wondered whether he might apologize for being so gruff when he awakened, if he remembered. She decided to write a long overdue letter to Connie, her college roommate. It was the first of a series of letters to Connie, but Kate did not mention her visits to Arlington Cemetery nor the problems of her marriage in any of them.

Connie read and reread Kate's last letter. It sounded despondent and Connie thought she knew why. "The girl's eating her heart out," she told her husband. "Remember, her first husband was killed in Vietnam? They only lived together a few days. I don't think she's ever gotten over it."

"After all these years? Wasn't it back in '68?"

"Yes, during the TET Offensive, if that was in '68." She looked at her husband sternly. Her eyes narrowed. "Bill, I don't find that so strange—it was so perfect, so ideal for both of them.

Connie's surgeon husband put down his newspaper, took off his glasses and gave the matter his full attention. "I s'pose. So, why not take her back to Bad Tölz and make her face the fact that he's gone? Evidently she hasn't faced it yet."

Connie gave him a worried look. "Sounds like your surgical knife at work. Would that be wise?"

His face was serious. "Well, in my opinion it's a radical treatment, but after so many years, probably the only cure."

"How on earth am I going to get her to go back? The girl does have a mind of her own!"

"Should be obvious," Bill replied. "Tell her you've always wanted to take a trip to Bavaria and ask her to go along. You would especially appreciate her company because she knows the area so well."

"She'll ask why you aren't going with me."

Bill shrugged. "Just say I'm too busy."

"Suppose Ivan wants to go?"

Bill was getting impatient. He sighed. "I don't think you need to worry. He won't want to travel around with two women, will he?"

"No, I guess not. But I'm not going to finagle this over the telephone! I'm going for a visit." She sat down at her desk and wrote Kate a letter that did not tell its real purpose. The letter began, "I've got a wonderful idea!" There was no hint what that meant.

When the letter arrived, Kate decided to call her, but Connie just laughed and said, "Wait and see. I'll tell you about my wonderful idea when I get there, that is, if I'm not interfering with your plans—yours and Ivan's. Just say so."

"Of course not. Hurry on down here. How about tomorrow? I want to know what you've got up your sleeve! And anyway, I want to see you. It's been a long time."

"Not tomorrow. How about the next day? I'll take Amtrak. I forget when it arrives in D.C. No use you fighting traffic. I'll take a cab."

Ivan had spent the day on the tennis court and was taking a shower when Connie paid off the taxi in front of the house. Kate dashed down the walk to grab her bag and pull her inside. "It's been too damn long," they both agreed and giggled. "That's what we always say——," "because it's true," the other one added. They had always finished each other's sentences.

A few minutes later, they saw Ivan on the stair landing above them. His wet hair was slicked back. "Do I hear girlish laughter?" Ivan joked, smiling at them. He came downstairs and greeted Connie warmly, the perfect host. "Nice to meet you after hearing about Connie all these years. You've got Kate all a twitter. Better tell us about this wonderful idea of yours ASAP." And to Kate, "By the way, where is my beer?"

"Let her get settled first before the interrogation! And your beer is in the refrigerator, where it always is."

Kate led Connie off to her room. "See how she treats me," called Ivan after them, and they heard the refrigerator door open. Connie listened to this exchange with interest. "Is he always so on edge?"

"No, just when he's tired," Kate assured her. She led Connie to her room. "What's new in your life? How's Bill? Too bad he couldn't come with you." She was talking too fast.

After dinner they sat in the den, the two women with cups of coffee, Ivan drinking a glass of Scotch. Ice clinked in his glass. He seemed to have lost interest in Connie's idea and was tapping the small table beside his chair, impatient with his companions and their conversation about college days. "It's now or never," thought Connie and plunged in, squinting at Kate over her cup. "I've kept you in suspense too long. Here's my idea. Wouldn't it be great if

we took a trip to Bavaria and especially to Bad
Tölz? I never got a chance to visit you all the
years you were there. You could show me the
places you wrote about in your letters."

Kate hesitated. She looked at Ivan but he
turned away and neither she nor Connie could
see his expression. His fingers drummed on the
table. "Go on if you want to," he said to no one
in particular and stood up.

"Will you come too?" Kate ventured. Connie
held her breath.

Ivan left the room to refill his glass and they
heard a decisive "No" followed by a more
friendly "not this time. Go ahead and enjoy
yourselves." He came back. "Maybe my former
secretary and her husband will invite me over
for dinner now and then while you're gone."

"Are you sure she has one?"

"One what?"

"Husband."

"Would I tell you if she didn't?"

They were back on safe ground, but Connie
worried until Ivan excused himself to go to bed.
"How about Ivan's secretary?" She avoided
Kate's eyes.

Her friend laughed. She sounded like the
lively girl Connie had known during their college days. "Oh, she's married all right. They
have five children—a very nice family."

"Well, that's good." Connie's face cleared.
"Let's plan the trip. When shall we go?"

Kate made up her mind on the spot, decided
it couldn't be put off any longer—way past time
to go back to Germany alone and face the past—
knife out her obsession with Jim, no matter how
painful. She had wrestled with it too long—time
to save her sanity and let Ivan go native if that's
what he wanted. After some discussion they
made definite plans.

While Connie stayed in Washington, Kate
invited Helen to meet them at the National
Gallery and the three had lunch together. They

were in the middle of a rather meager helping of Waldorf salad when they told Helen about their plans for a trip to Bavaria. Helen reacted with her usual lack of discretion. "Why isn't Ivan going with you?"

"Because he doesn't want to," Kate snapped. Realizing how it sounded, she added more pleasantly, "You know how he says he's had enough of living out of a suitcase."

Helen stopped just in time before she could say, "And why would he want to go along, you dummy?"

That night she told Dave she should have said it. "Might wake her up."

"What's the use? She's too far gone, poor Kate—still can't forget Jim even after all these years!"

"Poor Ivan!" his wife shot back and turned out the light. "Does it strike you Kate's not the old Kate we knew?"

Dave put his arms around her, pulling her close. "We all change, love. The hell with it! Forget both of em!"

CHAPTER TWENTY-SIX

Ivan yanked back the drapes in the den and stood at the window, already feeling a sense of loss. Yellow and brown leaves along the Potomac had begun to flutter slowly down in the drift of cool nights. The street lined with red maples in front of Kate and Ivan's house was changing into a 4-alarm blaze. He had picked up Connie at the Amtrak station an hour ago. The next evening he would take Kate and Connie to the airport to catch their flight to Munich.

A large black crow settled down heavily on the branch of a holly bush, rocking, arranging its wings neatly, head jerking in its quest for beetles. Ivan watched the crow. Begonia beds would soon droop in the early fall sun. No use watering them. They were going to die anyway. Ivan remembered what Kate had said when he suggested planting roses in the borders. "Roses don't do well in this sticky Washington heat and anyway, they have too many thorns." She had said it with an intensity and finality that hardly fit the circumstances. She should know he didn't really care what she planted.

From upstairs he heard her calling, "Ivan, come help me get this bag off the top shelf." For a moment, his eyes half-closed, shoulders hunched, he stayed by the window, looking out. Then he left the den and climbed the steps, one hand on the railing, not bothering to answer.

The day of the departure was muggy, overcast with the smell of rain in the air. Bags were packed and with nothing more to do, they were all uneasy, watching the clock. Ivan took them to lunch in a small French restaurant but none of them were hungry. It was just as well. The portions were not large enough to suit Ivan. He stated loudly so the proprietor would be sure to hear, "You can be Goddamn sure I won't come back here! A canary would starve to death in this dump."

At home again, they had a few minutes for
Ivan to put their baggage in the car and to ask
each other, "Have you got your passport?
Where's your ticket? Did you remember to put
in that little book of addresses?" And there was
a moment of panic while Connie searched for
her traveler's checks. Ivan was already in the car
waiting. Kate handed him the house key and he
backed the car out of the driveway.

The airport was crowded with what seemed
to be the entire population of Washington and
Virginia. Ivan stopped as close to the entrance as
possible and signaled a skycap. He put a sizable
tip in the man's outstretched hand and told Kate
he'd meet them at the ticket counter in a few
minutes. Behind him a car's horn protested, but
Ivan sat long enough before moving on to watch
Kate in her new emerald green suit walking into
the building. Her long red hair was gathered in a
soft knot at the nape of her neck. A wavy strand
had escaped and made a path behind her ear. His
mouth tightened. She was always going away
from him. His foot went down on the gas pedal.

Inside, Kate and Connie dealt with their bags
and ticket check-in. They did not have long to
wait. Ivan strode in and spotted them near the
entrance. As he came toward them, Connie
exclaimed, "Your husband is so handsome! You
must lead an exciting life together."

"In a way," agreed Kate, not sure what
Connie meant. Would this journey bring them
closer together or send them even farther apart?

Ivan almost collided with a flock of
teenagers but at the last minute managed to
avoid them. He muttered something under his
breath, frowned at his watch. "Time to head for
the departure gate," and loped off ahead. On the
way through the concourse Connie stopped at a
newsstand to buy a magazine. While Ivan and
Kate went on more slowly toward the gate, he
put an arm around her shoulder. "There's going
to be a big ocean between us, Babe. Don't forget

to send me a postcard."

"I won't forget," Kate promised, swallowing a sudden unexplainable lump in her throat.

Connie caught up with them and started through security. Ivan put both arms around Kate. His goodby kiss was long and hard on her mouth. It was time to go. At the last point where she could still see him, she felt tears in her eyes and waved. She saw him wave back with a big sweep of his arm. Then he turned and limped out of sight.

Connie and Kate stashed their extra possessions in the overhead compartment and along with other passengers, fastened seatbelts and settled into their seats. The plane rolled down the runway on its way to the Atlantic, and sunset faded behind them. Kate pictured Ivan going home to an empty house. He was probably mixing himself a drink, or more likely, on the rocks. She turned to Connie. "Let's celebrate—drink a toast to my trip back home and your first introduction to Bavaria."

"Why not." Connie grinned. "I can't wait. Having you along is perfect. Do you remember your deutsch?"

The whiskey felt warm and reassuring in Kate's throat. "Of course!" she bragged.

She wrinkled her nose while the hostess served their meal covered with brown gravy. The plane flew into darkness. As soon as the lights were dimmed, Kate heaved a sigh of relief. The goodbyes were over and they were on their way. Almost immediately she fell into a deep sleep. Connie read until the movie began, but she too went to sleep before it ended.

The sun woke them up over the Channel. Lines to the lavatories filled the aisles and they barely had time to freshen up before the plane went into its landing pattern. Kate thought, "Here I am again. Is Germany still home? Will I be cured or is my life going to keep going downhill?" She began to shake. They were on the runway. Her hands trembled so much; Connie had to help her pull her carry-on bag out of the overhead compartment.

Inside the airport they fought their way through a crush of passengers. It seemed like an eternity before baggage from their plane began to appear on the carrousel, but finally they corralled their bags and struggled into line for customs. "Why did I bring so much stuff?" Connie gasped. They fished out passports and pushed their baggage along with their feet.

Past the barrier Kate's eyes sparkled and her face flushed with pleasure. Snatches of German conversations were like old friends and German signs pointed to the bus into town. "I'm home!" she shouted, causing several people nearby to smile.

"Hey, wait for me!" Connie had dropped her purse and was juggling her passport, luggage, and raincoat, trying to pick it up. Kate gave her a hand and they found the bus into Munich, giving the driver their baggage to lift on board. Kate's eyes were glued to the bus window as they rode into the city and she exclaimed at every familiar landmark.

Their hotel near the opera was in the center of Munich, small, comfortable with a touch of luxury. Kate explained they could walk to almost all the main sights tourists see—"and some others that most of them miss."

"Let's throw our stuff in the room and begin!"

"Yeah! I'm ready! We'll stop at the desk and get a few deutschmarks—not too many. Banks give a better exchange."

"Okay, guide. Don't lose me," Connie laughed. "I hope you remember your German."

"It's a little rusty but never mind. It will come back. Just remember how to say "Grüss Gott" and you'll be all right. Most Germans speak at least some English. They learn it in school."

Outside the hotel they turned toward the chic shopping area around the opera, walking briskly but stopping to stare in store window displays. "Wow! Prices have really gone up!" Kate did some mental calculations. "See that simple little dress? It costs about $450 in U.S. dollars."

Connie clutched her purse tight. "How can the locals afford prices like that? Some of them must have big bucks." She could not tear herself away from a dress in one of the windows with seed pearls sewn all over the bodice.

"Come on." Kate dragged her down a side street. "Let's have a beer at the Hofbrauhaus. You won't believe it." It was early evening and lights were coming on. The sound of an oompah band poured out of the wide doors. They were pushed inside by a throng of tourists and Germans, jostled by buxom Bavarian waitresses in Dirndls carrying three or more foaming Steins of beer in each hand. The noise was deafening.

Kate remembered the Saturday so long ago when she and Ivan and Hunk and Jim had driven to Munich for a night on the town. They had spent hours sharing a long table in the Hofbrauhaus with a group of Germans, former prisoners of war in Russia. They had all been so happy.

Connie nudged Kate and pointed at the occupants of a bench by one of the long tables. A little brown and white dog of mixed ancestry sat on its haunches between two portly Bavarians in Lederhosen who took turns offering the dog a sip of their beer. Kate managed a smile. In spite of her best efforts, the smile turned into a yawn.

Even after their long journey and a day of sightseeing, Connie was not ready to give up. Finally, above the noise of the band and hundreds of merrymakers, Kate shouted in her ear, "We'll come back another day."

Outside the building Connie turned to Kate with a startled expression. "Did you see those waitresses dipping Steins in and out of a tub of cold water to wash them?"

Kate did her best again to smile. "I guess the beer has so much alcohol it kills all the germs."

Trying to put out of her mind what was ahead, Kate spent a restless night. By morning, jet lag had turned into ordinary fatigue, but she summoned enough strength to pull herself out of bed. Connie was already in the shower, full of energy and ready to go. Kate groaned.

After a continental breakfast in the hotel, the first event on the agenda, booked the night before, was a tour of the National Theater and the Residenz, home of Bavarian kings until 1918. After Kate and Connie came out of the palace, Kate pointed down the street to a wrought iron gate. "You'll love this!" Inside was a formal courtyard and the Cuvilliés Theater, its ornate interior so intimately small and extravagantly Baroque that it always transported Kate to the time of Mozart. While the guide talked, she let her mind go back to the operas she had seen there. Other memories not connected to Mozart's music crept in.

The guide finished talking and Connie marveled, "This looks just like a red velvet jewel box full of gold and diamonds!"

"Come on. We'll be late for the Glockenspiel." Kate pulled Connie's arm and they reached Marienplatz, the true center of the city, just as the clock began to chime and the figures of knights in the tower of the city hall started the jousting that draws crowds every day at eleven o'clock.

"Look at me, standing here with my mouth open just like the rest of the tourists."

Kate meant to share her friend's enthusiasm, but there was a wistful note in her words. "I must admit I'm not as impressed as the first time I saw it, but why turn blasé? It's still fun, and I haven't seen it for such a long time."

They wandered out of Marienplatz in the direction of the Hauptbahnhof. The street was

wide, reserved for pedestrians, bordered by
stores. A warm sun shone on crowds of people,
flower and vegetable carts and elderly Germans
enjoying the fresh air. Groups sat around fountains while children played hide and seek with
rainbow jets of water.

A carnival spirit seemed to color everyone
and everything in the street. Young men with
long hair juggled plates, scattered leaflets, and
exhorted audiences who came, listened a few
brief moments and moved on to the next attrac-
tion.

In front of Connie and Kate a young woman
strummed a mournful tune on her guitar. Her
Dachshund wriggled impatiently at her feet.
Each time she stopped playing, the dog's long
nose pushed a cup containing a few deutschmark
toward customers. They put in some coins and
went on their way. The sad music followed them
and Kate's mouth quivered. "I should have come
over here with Ivan when I had the chance."

Connie tried to be matter-of-fact. "You can
still come another time. Listen, Kate, I'm getting
hungry. Do you know a place?"

"Sure do, if it's still here. The best
Nürnberger sausages and sauerkraut you'll ever
eat." She led Connie around the corner to a quiet
square. A few small tables had been set out in
front of a building that had either survived
World War II or been restored to its original
Medieval appearance. They chose a table that
had just been vacated.

Kate hung her sweater over her chair. "Such
unusual weather for November. It should be
raining." Doves stepped daintily around their
feet, pecking at crumbs; a few stragglers from a
nearby thoroughfare strolled by; twin domes of
the Frauenkirche towered above them, and they
heard a subdued jumble of the hectic bustle a
block away.

The waiter brought a basket of fresh hard
rolls and pungent sausages on a heap of sauer-

kraut aromatic with juniper berries. Connie attacked her food with both fork and knife in the European custom. Kate cut a bite-size piece of sausage, her thoughts far away. "Aren't you hungry?" Connie asked.

"Oh yes." Kate put the morsel of meat in her mouth. She fiddled with her food, at the end of the meal, leaving her plate only half eaten.

Connie made up her mind. "Okay, I know you're anxious to go back to Bad Tölz. Why don't you go tomorrow? I'll go along if you need company, but I'd be just as happy to stay here, take some city tours and browse around the shops. Up to you." She added, "I do want to see Bad Tölz. Later, before we head home, you can take me along and show me the town I've heard so much about."

Kate reached across the table and touched Connie's hand. "You're so understanding. No wonder I've always loved you. Yes, if you really wouldn't mind, I need to go alone this first time. I won't be gone but a day or two."

"It's settled then. Don't worry about me. Everybody speaks English and I'll get along fine, rummage around the antique shops by the river, and maybe visit the Deutsches Museum. Just call me from time to time."

"I know somebody you can get in touch with in a pinch," Kate assured her. "One of our teachers married a German. They live in Harlaching on the edge of Munich. I'll call her tonight and leave you her name and phone number. You'd like her."

"Not necessary but thanks, girl. You think of everything."

CHAPTER TWENTY-SEVEN

Early on what promised to be a fine fall day, but cool, Kate drove south along the Autobahn, alone. She turned off on a secondary road. Soon she saw the airstrip and just beyond it the school on the outskirts of Bad Tölz.

It was almost unbearable—a mistake to come back. Kate gripped the steering wheel hard and drove her rented VW slowly past the American Dependents School where her third graders had watched the Green Berets float down to the airstrip, parachutes drifting above them. Now only ghosts rode the air. Windows of Flint Kaserne were coming up on her left, vacant and secretive after years of intense activity inside its walls. The 10th Special Forces Group, Airborne was gone and the Kaserne looked eerily like a deserted prison, no longer the Green Berets' only European base—the place where she had said goodby to Jim. Not goodby—I love you—were the words she'd said. She remembered exactly.

Leaving Washington, Kate had taken Jim's diamond solitaire off the gold chain around her neck and put it on her left hand. Now it flamed red and green sparks as if it caught the sun, but there was no sun. The lump of dry tears crowding her throat was getting heavier. Flashes of memory brought moments she had almost forgotten.

In the late Fifties a 5mph speed limit was posted on the Kaserne gate. A Green Beret officer once registered disapproval by getting out of his car and pushing it through the entrance, an act of defiance that quickly made the rounds of the 10th. Not that they were averse to rules, but rules were required to meet certain high standards, the most basic being survival. Their commanders had no quarrel with that.

One icy winter's night long ago it was an ordeal to drive up the hill to this gate. There was

the horrible possibility that the car might get
stuck at the stoplight and the MP at the gate
would discover a senior officer on the floor in
the back seat, out of uniform as it were.

That evening had started like many others
after the teachers moved inside the Kaserne,
with supper cooking in the kitchen. It was
almost done when the doorbell rang. She opened
the door and saw, framed in whirling snow, a
senior officer whose wife had thrown him out
clad only in his pink underwear. With him was a
young lieutenant passing by who realized this
was one of his bosses and should be rescued. Of
course, she invited them to supper after which
they all thought it would be a good joke to visit
friends down the hill in the housing area. In fact,
she reflected, the evening had been a roaring
success. Life was full of unexpected fun—then.

Flashing lights from a Mercedes inches
behind her VW awoke Kate to the fact that the
stoplight had changed to green. Forgetting her
VW didn't have automatic shift, she stalled the
engine and before she could start it, the light
changed back to red. The Mercedes driver threw
up his hands in despair.

Clouds began to darken the sky. The mournful November day suited her mood. She was
glad Connie had stayed in Munich, letting her
come alone to Bad Tölz. So many windows in
her life had opened here. Connie had had no part
in those years and Kate wanted for this one day
to think about Camelot—the penumbra of
urgency, the closeness that was more than the
usual military brotherhood, an elite grown-up
boys' club where the Green Berets played
games—serious, silly, happy games between
wars, teasing and insulting each other like brothers. Growing old wasn't part of the plan. Kate
wondered briefly what Ivan was doing in D.C.—
probably drinking too much while she was
away. "There's nothing I can do about that," she
said loudly, startled at the sound of her voice.

Kate found her way through a complexity of new roads across the river to the Badeteil part of Bad Tölz and the place where the Park Hotel used to be. A retirement home stood there now and all traces of the old hotel in the Fifties were gone. The streets were crowded with cars, but she nudged the VW into a parking place and walked back to a bench across from the retirement home feeling a kind of lassitude. It wasn't such a good idea to come back. Better to leave the past blurred than try to focus it in cutting outlines. Do the old people living here have crazy dreams still surviving from Green Beret days?

A light gust of wind rubbed bare branches against each other and stirred a puddle of old leaves in front of Kate. The clouds darkening the day broke apart into a flock of wooly white sheep with gray undersides wandering from the foothills of the Alps northward toward Munich. It was cool and Kate pulled her coat together under her chin. The air stirred again and shook around her, then became very still. The walls of the new building in front of her knew she was there, had been there once before their time in this place. She could feel her heart beating.

Half closing her eyes to shut out the new building, she began to feel the essence of place, the soft, cool air, the wet smell of grass after rain, weak rays of sunshine between passing clouds. Unrelated pieces came back like children who had never grown up—stories still repeated when the originals met up with old friends who had been there and remembered—clinging to the hope their stories would not be forgotten.

What was the name of the slightly drunk lieutenant from Arkansas who knocked on my door, when Jane and I were planning a trip to Berchtesgaden? "Come on in, Tommy," I said.

He just stood there glassy-eyed, very polite, "Come with me girls. I've got something to show you."

"What, Tommy?"

"Can't tell you. It's in my room."

"It's been a long day with the little darlings, Tommy. How about tomorrow?"

"No, now," he entreated, looking pathetic.

"Oh all right, but make it snappy." We went across the hall to his room where he tucked us in bed with all our clothes on including shoes, and told long garbled stories about Humpty Dumpty and The Three Bears. When he nodded off in his chair we tried to sneak off, but he woke up and pleaded with us not to go home. Sometime after midnight we finally tiptoed away to our own rooms. It would have been a shame to upset him! He's such a nice fellow.

A passerby glanced at Kate curiously, thinking she must be an American—those shoes. But you really couldn't tell these days. Lots of Europeans looked like Americans—something to do with Hollywood—not a good thing! Lost in her thoughts, Kate didn't notice the man's interest. She still looked much as she had more than twenty years before. Her face had softened but the good bone structure was still there and her dark auburn hair had only a little gray. There was a quality of eagerness, of waiting for something, that made strangers wonder who she was, where she was going, what she was thinking to make her smile.

Kate found herself humming a song from the Fifties under her breath, hating the tune—tiresome, and a monotony of humming. She tried desperately to think of other music, but couldn't escape the insistent tune in her head like an exasperating clown doing somersaults in a graveyard. Had the building in front of her and its occupants captured her mind?

Kate straightened and then stood up, hesitating. "Here I'm whining, in my old hometown—going to be a wonderful day." Without any warning, her eyes overflowed with tears stinging

like a touch of ammonia. I shouldn't have come
back. Or else I shouldn't have gone away—turning into a damn crybaby! Jim, dearest Jim, I've
changed so much you wouldn't know me now. I
can't cope. What in God's name am I going to
do?

Hastily Kate put on her sunglasses. They
made the clouds even darker than before, but at
least hid her reddened eyes from passersby. She
wandered across the bridge and up Marktstrasse
wondering why the street seemed so steep.
Memory played tricks. Many of the shops she
knew were gone, replaced by tourist oddities
that didn't belong here, and hidden behind the
painted facades in this postcard town on the
edge of the Alps. There was the top hat sign still
hanging outside the hatmaker's shop like an old
friend. At least some of the people were still
wearing traditional Bavarian clothes. She
noticed a man in Lederhosen coming toward her
with a grin on his ruddy bearded face. It was one
of the school bus drivers. "Miss O'Brien!
Remember me?"

"Of course," she said, trying to think of his
name. They hugged each other and she was
home again in the Isar Valley, its unchanging
mountains, and the milk-jade river beginning its
long way to the Black Sea. Ivan should be here.
This was his town too, and I shouldn't have
come without him.

The bus driver went on his way, turning back
and waving as he disappeared into a shop. She
passed a bookstore with postcards by the door. A
view of the Isar Valley looking south to the
mountains caught her eye. It was the symbol of
everything she loved about Bad Tölz and so
popular there was only one left. She paid for it
and dashed off a message to Ivan,
"Remembering good times—wishing you were
here to remember with me. Love, Kate." Oddly,
she did wish Ivan were there.

The feeling followed her back to the

Badeteil, and she decided to call Connie and postpone her return to Munich. She would drive to Garmisch, find a room for the night and spend the day there. She'd see if she could cut out the part of her that still brought her to tears at unexpected moments—totally inappropriate tears after so many years. She hadn't played fair with Ivan, hanging on to her old grief.

It would be crowding her luck to stay at the Eibsee. Maybe some place in Unterammergau. She chose the old narrow winding road, now almost a lane. There was hardly any traffic except for a herd of cows heading back to the barn. She found a room just before early dark when the light suddenly plunged behind the mountains bringing loneliness so harsh she felt like the only survivor in an empty world. She tried to eat and lingered in the little dining area, reading German newspapers and drinking a beer until she felt tired enough to go to bed and finally sleep.

Her dreams were crowded with strange surreal illusions. Helen was throwing ice cubes around at a party, substituting lighted matches when Dave objected, calling him the most horrible names she could think of. In Kate's dream, third graders were holding hands, standing in a circle around them, watching.

Her dreams changed, became more grotesque, threatening. She was in a jungle and Jim was coming, but he walked by without seeing her. She tried but couldn't call to him and thick vines tripped her, holding her feet. Ivan dropped down beside her, stony-faced, saying very seriously, "The—sky—is—falling." She reached frantically for his jump boots to pull herself loose, but the parachute took him back up above the treetops into a red cloud full of blackbirds. Kate struggled desperately to free herself from the tangle of vines and woke up, her heart pounding. The bedclothes were wound around her feet like a vise.

The day began—a strange day. She had come to Europe to find Jim, but Ivan was somehow taking over her thoughts. She wondered again what he was doing. Ivan was easily bored, craving action, moving around rooms like a caged lion, testing perimeters and trying the exits. He was always the most aggravating when he was miserable. Poor Ivan. She must try to recover the camaraderie—the closeness—they had in the old days in Bad Tölz and when they traveled together. "He's changed so much and face it, yes, face it! You've changed even more." With an effort she turned her mind back to Jim, picked up her overnight bag and went out to the car.

CHAPTER TWENTY-EIGHT

Kate drove slowly south, reluctant to go toward the past still burning inside her. After coming this far she had to go on. The last miles slipped by, and she entered Garmisch Partenkirchen on the road dividing the two towns. New one-way streets had changed the area so much; she lost her sense of direction and couldn't find the Billeting Office. Perhaps it was no longer in the same place. Garmisch had grown much larger since she last saw its main street meandering through town like a country lane.

Confused, Kate took her bearings from the position of the Zugspitze and the Alpspitze. At least the mountains were in the same place! She drove up to the Eibsee cable car station and went into the hotel but recognized nothing. The German owners had renovated it and the configuration of the lobby was different than the old entrance. Rooms still faced the lake and the desk clerk asked if she wanted to see one of them. "Maybe tomorrow." she answered in German and fled to the car. But she must make herself walk by the lake down the same path. Halfway measures wouldn't cure her. Even though it was cool and out-of-season, a few German couples were strolling along the path. A hundred yards from the hotel, Kate began to feel nauseated and turned around, retracing her steps to the car.

Wallgau was the next stop Kate had planned, but she didn't feel up to it. She had tried many times to bring back the details of her time with Jim, but the only part she could remember was their goodbye. Now it was coming back to her precisely, painfully. Then the picture in her mind blurred and the reality of Ivan blotted out Jim's words. She'd tried so hard to make a life, but it had turned out a wasteland—not Ivan's fault, more likely hers, she thought with a pang, remembering the time he brought her a dozen red roses after one of his drunks. She'd put them in a vase that was too small and walked out of the room quickly, before the smell made her sick. His voice followed her, contrite, saying he was sorry, really sorry, and finally, "Je-e-esus Chr-rist! What does a guy have to do? Get down on his knees?" She wasn't upset because he'd been drinking. She knew it and he knew it, but neither of them could say it out loud.

The years hadn't been all bad—mostly good when they were with a group of oldtimers trading stories, when they traveled together overseas, and sometimes when she pretended hard enough. And they still enjoyed the same music, the same arguments, and the same books. She was growing older. Ivan felt young when he was drinking.

Kate came back to her surroundings. She was surprised to find she had driven up to Oberammergau past all those hairpin curves on a rain-slicked road and hadn't the faintest idea how she got there. "What's the matter with me?" Her hands were shaking and she promised herself she would watch the road, think about what she was doing, not let her mind wander for a second. Jim had been gone for such a long time, and even this trip to the past wasn't helping her live without him. It was a never-ending ache and in the old surroundings it was even worse.

The trees were dripping from a fine misty rain the Bavarians call Schnurregen. Low clouds covered the rocky heights and uplands. Now she was near the center of town, passing the Red Riding Hood house. The painted pictures on its walls had always fascinated her, but today she gave them only a passing glance. She had valid excuses for not going in the restaurant where she and Jim had eaten. It was getting late; she was tired; and anyway she wasn't sure she could bear it.

Kate stopped the car in front of the restaurant, indecisive, cold, feeling the dampness in her bones. She decided to go in after all and have a hot bowl of goulash soup. After parking the car on one of the side streets near the Passion Play Theater and walking back, she discovered the restaurant was closed until six o'clock. She didn't feel like waiting that long. "Or maybe," she muttered to herself, "I just can't take it any more. I'm doing the weak sister act that I've always despised in other people."

A fenced-in corner of her mind had known for a long time that she was self-destructing, eaten, devoured by obsessive longing for Jim, taking Ivan down with her. But the knowledge had been pushed far away, where she wouldn't have to think about it, or do something about it—until now. She'd made the best of it and that had probably been the worst of it. So many wasted years! She felt suddenly old and disoriented. What difference did it really make? The trip had been too long and she felt very tired. She drove back to the Pension and gathered up her belongings.

The day was ending. Kate started back toward Munich on the direct highway. She decided to stop in Murnau to get something to eat and called Connie to tell her she'd be back in the city in about an hour and a half.

"You sound funny, Kate. Are you all right?"

"Yes, I'm fine. Just a little tired."

"Maybe you should stay there in Murnau tonight and come back in the morning."

"No, I'll be careful. See you in a little while."

Kate didn't feel like eating after all and realized she was in a highly emotional state. She wondered if she should follow Connie's advice and stay in Murnau for the night, but she went out to the car and drove out on the main road. The traffic was moving too fast on wet slippery roads. She would need to drive cautiously, especially since it was still raining and the reflection of lights on the pavement was confusing. She peered through the sweep of windshield wipers, her hands tense, gripping the steering wheel.

It was not her fault. She saw the headlights of an on-coming car and was well over on her own side of the road, but the BMW was traveling too fast for the curve on a rainy night and smashed head-on into Kate's small car. According to the official police report, she never regained consciousness and died in the Starnberg Hospital at 11:55 P.M.

That night the lights around Eibsee dimmed and went out. The sudden darkness and shutters banging in the wind awakened a young British couple that was vacationing at the Eibsee Hotel. They opened the shutters and looked out into blackness. The wind was rising, twisting dark treetops, tossing whitecaps dimly visible on the lake's surface and driving streamers of mist along the water's edge. The flicker of color, like a diamond catching the sun, was so tiny they didn't remember it afterward. Lights came on again, and they saw two figures in the distance walking hand in hand, their heads bent into the west wind. The English couple watched until they disappeared around a curve in the path.

A sudden gust, a river of cold air, poured into the room. He forced the window shut and they crept into bed seeking the warmth of each other's arms, wondering what two people were doing out so late on such a cold windy night. The contact of their bodies was unexpected, different, as if they had never known each other before. The travel clock said midnight.

Connie finally reached Ivan in D.C.—he'd been out with the boys and was sleeping it off. There was a long moment of silence and she thought the connection had been broken, but then he told her he'd wire money and come over if she needed him. She said the Consulate would help her handle things. Ivan could hear her crying. He sent money, called a friend at the Munich Consulate, and made necessary arrangements. Then he got out a bottle of Scotch and deliberately and systematically drank one straight shot after another, until somewhere in his brain he heard Devorian say, "She belongs to me, you know, ol' man." Ivan passed out blotto drunk.

When he didn't show up at the health club, his friends came and took away all his liquor until they were sure he could handle himself. At his age, they told each other, he could easily drink himself to death. Kate's postcard from Bad Tölz came a week later. Ivan read it twice and opened another bottle of scotch. Drinking had never before sent him into a crying jag.

When the west wind blows at midnight over the Eibsee, two dim figures are sometimes seen in the distance walking along the lakeshore. Through time they have become a legend—a legend with no known beginning.

The original Green Berets who survived, retired and still played games around the globe for oddball organizations based in D.C. Some sold real estate in Myrtle Beach and Scottsdale; some are listed on the Vietnam Memorial; one who helped liberate Dachau succumbed to Alzheimer's disease and two who seemed particularly sane committed suicide. Shot and badly wounded by a jealous ex-husband, Colonel Peter Gulden let himself bleed to death rather than face living half a life.

As years went by, adjustment to civilian life became easier for the original Green Berets. In these late years the few who are left, live and die like ordinary men. Somewhere in soldier heaven the ones who are gone still play jokes and borrow socks from each other without asking, just as they used to do in the Park Hotel. The world they knew in Tölz so long ago was a stopping place, a surrogate home painted in vivid antic colors, the central anecdote in a fable between the wars they won and the wars they lost.

The designated patch was created and designed by
Harris Munck and *William Hamel* for the Vietnamese
Ranger Airborne assigned to the CIA base camps of
Bien Hoa and Hoa Cam in Viet Nam, July 1961.